A JEWISH GIRL
IN THE
WEIMAR REPUBLIC

A JEWISH GIRL
IN THE
WEIMAR REPUBLIC

BY STEPHANIE ORFALI

Ronin Publishing
Box 1035
Berkeley, California 94701

Published by:
Ronin Publishing, Inc.
Post Office Box 1035
Berkeley, California 94701

A Jewish Girl in the Weimar Republic
ISBN: 0-914171-10-0

First printing 1987
Printed in the United States of America

Project editor: Sebastian Orfali
Manuscript editor: Nancy Krompotich
Developmental editors: Jim Schreiber and Sebastian Orfali
Keyboarding: Iris Miller, Nancy Krompotich
Cover Design: Brian Groppe
Text layout and pasteup: Howard Munson
Typography by Nickel Ads and Generic Typography

ACKNOWLEDGMENTS

First of all, I want to thank my husband Jacob and our son Sebastian for all their help. Without Sebastian's prodding, coaching and advice this autobiography would never have been written.

Second, I want to thank Milton Lott and his Autobiography writing class at the Napa Valley College, who listened to most of the stories and helped with their comments, questions and advice.

Thirdly, I want to thank Nancy Krompotich, my devoted editor, who brought order to my sometimes confused narrative.

And finally, I want to give thanks to the photo archive of the City of Nuernberg for the beautiful pictures of Nuernberg.

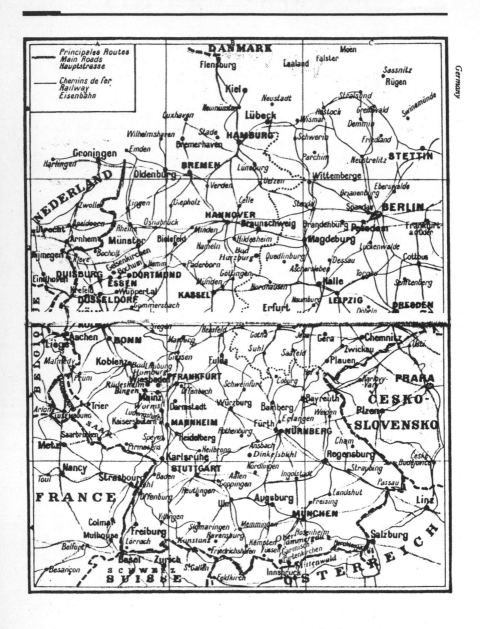

Contents

Introduction

I have read numerous books about the horrors of the concentration camps, but the books about the Jewish young people of my own generation are scarce. We were between 18 and 22 years old when Hitler began his rule that finally left 6 million Jews dead in unnamed graves.

We had finished our school years, but were not yet established in our professions, and had not yet acquired assets that we did not want to leave behind. We were free to emigrate and are now scattered all over the world. But we are haunted by memories that will not go away.

I am trying to capture a childhood that was lived sitting on a volcano that finally erupted. Yet, it was a childhood and adolescence during which we, our family, and our friends shared and loved the rich culture of our homeland that rejected us, during which most of us enjoyed the amenities of affluence, and became gradually aware of our Jewish heritage, which had to sustain us, when hatred was showered upon us.

This book is about the personal experiences of my family, our friends, and myself, as well as about the events that led to the ascendence of Adolf Hitler during the years of the ill-fated Weimar Republic.

The events and places are true as I remember them, and as accurate as I was able to verify them through souvenirs, diaries,

View from the Castle of Nuernberg.

The city of Nuernberg in ruins.

and pictures. The historical data have been checked and I hope they are correct. I have changed some of the names, but not all.

Eight thousand Jews were living in Nuernberg in 1933 (1.8% of the population). At the beginning of World War II, most of them had left Nuernberg but 2,539 remained. Of these, 1,631 were deported to concentration camps. Seventy-two of them survived.

Nuernberg lay in ruins in 1945 but has since been rebuilt, reproducing the old, medieval splendor.

The city rebuilt.

The reconstructed street and castle.

MÜNCHS & WALTER   NÜRNBERG.

Emilie as a young girl.

I. My Grandmother, Emilie

My great-grandfather, David Ottensooser was a painter. He kept a diary between 1840 and 1843 when he studied painting in Munich and Dresden.

In this diary we read that he was a very unhappy man who resented his poverty, who was aware that his talent was limited, and who immersed himself in self-pity and unrequited love affairs.

He had to give up his ambition to become a famous painter of large historical tableaus, because his family needed his help. He married a wealthy woman, Adelheid Bloch. With her dowry, he acquired a small porcelain factory and passed his time as a porcelain painter. Painting was still his hobby, and we cherish a lovely painting of David and his wife Adelheid.

David and Adelheid had three children, Wilhelm, Eugen and Emilie. They all were born in the large house of the factory in the center of Baiersdorf, a small Bavarian town which David describes lovingly in his diary.

David died as a young man, when his daughter Emilie was ten years old. Adelheid moved to Nuernberg, where she lived in an ancient house in the old city near the castle, on top of the hill where Emilie had a splendid view of the city with which she fell in love. Emilie never told us stories about her childhood, but we have a class picture taken during her years in a private girls' high school, where she sits poorly dressed among her elaborately garbed classmates.

She grew up in the shadow of her wealthy Bloch cousins, wearing their hand-me-downs as the poor orphan girl. She was very pretty, with delicate features and golden hair, probably strawberry blonde as her children said, though she told me that she had flaming red hair as I had.

Emilie loved to recite poetry and was always chosen to recite during school celebrations. She also loved to sing. She had a clear, resonant soprano voice, and used to sing solos in the choir of the synagogue. When she sang the whole building was filled into the furthest corners with her bell-like voice.

The Synagogue.

When Emilie was a young woman, a famous impresario visited Nuernberg and attended services in the synagogue. He was deeply impressed by Emilie's singing, realizing that he had discovered the great soprano of his time. He went up to the choir and asked to be introduced to her. When he saw the beautiful girl, he imagined himself as her manager on concert and opera stages throughout the world.

Right after the services, he went to the house of his nightingale. He told her mother, "Give me this girl and I will make a second Jenny Lind of her."

Emilie listened behind a closed door with a pounding heart.

Adelheid answered, "I have to talk to her guardian before I can decide anything." Emilie shivered with excitement. She saw herself on a concert stage, belting out the soprano aria from Beethoven's Ninth Symphony that she was studying as a member of the "Verein fuer den klassischen Chorgesant," the society for classical choral singing.

Then she heard her mother say, "Emilie is so young. There is plenty of time to start her studies."

"No," said the impresario. "If she wants to be really great, she has to start now."

After he had left, a flushing Emilie begged her mother to see Uncle Samuel right away. What a splendid occasion to escape her lot as the poor orphan girl!

Samuel's answer was a firm and final no. "No member of our respectable family will ever be an entertainer."

Adelheid said meekly, "Don't forget, David was a painter and she has his artist blood in her veins."

"And what became of him?" asked her brother sternly. "He ended up as an obscure porcelain painter who squandered your dowry on a bad business and left you a penniless widow in our care."

"The poor man never had a chance."

"No," said Samuel. "Emilie will grow up and get married. I will give her a nice dowry, but never ask me again that she should study music."

Emilie was heartbroken. The little bird had singed its wings before it even learned how to fly. She fell in love with the director of the choral society, but he was not Jewish and it was a hopeless situation because Samuel would never give his consent to a mixed marriage.

Throughout her adult life, she was a bitter and despondent woman, blaming Samuel for keeping her from the career she felt was her right, and later, trapped in a marriage that had been arranged by her guardian to a man she did not love.

After music, patriotism was Emilie's second passion. She was an ardent Bavarian. When Emilie was born, Germany was a conglomerate of numerous independent kingdoms, duchies, and free cities. Nuernberg, a former free city, was part of the kingdom of Bavaria and was ruled by Ludwig the First of Wittelsbach. He was succeeded in 1864 by 18 year old Ludwig II. Under his reign, Germany was united by Otto von Bismark under the leadership of the Prussian king, who became emperor Wilhelm I of Germany. Bavaria was still called a kingdom, but lost its independence. Emilie never forgave Prussia for robbing her country and its king of their independence.

Young king Ludwig was her idol, and she followed his career with fascination and despair. Pictures of his extravagant palaces and castles on which he squandered Bavarian taxpayer's money, adorned the walls of her tiny room, and she hummed arias of the Wagner operas because Richard Wagner was a friend of the king. Later, when the king had to end his friendship with Wagner on the urging of his ministers, who resented the huge amounts of money the king lavished on Wagner, she admitted that Wagner's music bored her to death, and that she sat through his interminable operas only because he was a friend of the king, but later she changed her mind about Wagner when he created the Meistersingers of Nuernberg, an opera that glorified her beloved Nurernberg.

In 1886 Ludwig II was declared insane and put under the care of a doctor. Two weeks later he and his doctor were found drowned in a lake near Munich.

When Emilie was 20 years old, Samuel decided that it was time to arrange a marriage for Emilie before she reached the age of 21 and would be able to choose an unsuitable husband for herself or, worse, run away to study music and bring the family into disgrace.

Nuernberg around 1900.

At that time, two brothers from West Prussia, Moriz and Arnold Bernhard had settled in Nuernberg and opened a wholesale business in men's hats and gloves. They were customers of the Bloch Bank, and Samuel invited them to his house as "Hausfreunde," friends of the family, as it was the custom at that time to invite bachelors into their homes, mostly to create closely supervised entertainment for their unmarried, sheltered daughters. Samuel's wife had second thoughts about this arrangement after Moriz, the older of the two brothers, married a wealthy society girl. She was afraid that one of her daughters might marry the other brother, whose social status as a merchant was below the status of the daughter of rich banker. Samuel found a way out of the dilemma by arranging a marriage between Emilie and Arnold. Arnold was in love with this pretty girl and he was also in need of money and Samuel gave his ward a nice dowry.

Emilie and Arnold were married a few days before Emilie's 21st birthday when the guardianship ended.

Soon after the marriage Arnold found out that his lovely wife had a nasty disposition; she hated Prussians. The two began to quarrel often and Emilie called him "Saupreusse."

One year after their marriage, Emilie gave birth to a little girl who died soon afterwards. To cheer her up, Arnold took his wife to see his parents. Johanna and Hirsch Bernhard lived in a rambling house in Tuchel, West Prussia, which would become Polish territory after World War I. Since their five children had left, the house was quite empty during the year, but during summer when many of their children and grand-children came to visit, the house reverberated with laughter and cheer. Besides the Bernhard clan there lived in Tuchel the large Kuttner and Cohn families with whom they had many family ties through marriage. I have never been able to sort the family out because two Kuttner brothers married two Cohn sisters, and marriages between cousins were frequent. Each member of the family was related to every other member at least through two common forefathers. Everybody called everybody cousin even if they were many times removed.

Emilie was very apprehensive on her first trip into enemy ter-ritory, but it was impossible for her not to enjoy the hustle and bustle in Tuchel that was such a contrast to her own lonely childhood when she grew up in genteel poverty without ever knowing her father, with an unhappy mother.

Arnold and Emilie crowned their trip with a stay in the

fashionable resort, Zoppoth, on the Baltic Sea. It was the first time that Emilie saw the sea. She ventured into the water in a coverall bathing suit, and she regretted that she could not swim.

The love of the sea remained with Emilie all through her life and created in her a longing for being able to swim that she was never able to achieve. I was the fortunate recipient of her desire for lessons when years later, as her grandchild, she insisted I take lessons at a municipal pool near her home.

On the train ride from Zoppoth to Nuernberg, she suffered from morning sickness. When the doctor confirmed her pregnancy, she was unhappy at the prospect of having a baby so soon after the tragedy of her first child, but she consoled herself that this time she would give birth to a son, a son who would serve the Bavarian king, though he was partly Prussian.

The pregnancy was difficult and Emilie barely left her home. She even gave up her membership in the choral society, which had been her solace during her adolescence.

Her daughter, Frieda, was born on a lovely spring day with the sun shining through the windows. She enjoyed the beautiful baby in spite of her disappointment that it was another girl.

However, she never had close ties to Frieda, who was fed by a wet nurse. Later, a nanny would take care of her while Emilie took up her social life again.

Not too long after Frieda's birth, Emilie again became pregnant. She was very depressed and spent most of the time lying on the sofa in the living room, leaving the household chores and the care for Frieda to her overworked maid.

Arnold tried in vain to get her on her feet, but all he got for his endeavors were bitter words of accusation for getting her pregnant again and for being a Saupreusse. When the next girl was born on April 20, 1882, Emilie rejected her completely. She did not even bother to give the child a name. Finally, two months later, she went herself to the civil registry to tell them that the girl was named Hedwig. During her infancy, Hedwig had polio, and her left side was slightly paralyzed, so that she was clumsy and walked with a limp. Frieda was a serious, precocious, and very attractive girl who used to look down upon her stupid, handicapped little sister.

More than a year passed without another pregnancy. Arnold's business improved and he rented a large, sunny apartment outside the city walls, near his business. It was on the first floor of a large apartment building with a tiny front garden. It was very spacious, with two wings, one for the living area and the other for bedrooms and bath. The two sections were separated by a glass door.

Emilie became pregnant for a fourth time, but during this pregnancy she was cheerful and busied herself with decorating her new home. They bought elaborate furniture for the formal dining room. It was in neo-Gothic style. The buffet had an elaborately carved, altarlike structure with little spires and many shelves full of knick-knacks that had to be dusted constantly. The living room was in dark oak. It also contained a rosewood piano and the sofa that was Emilie's refuge in times of misery or just plain laziness. A bay window in this living room contained two rocking chairs, a simple rattan chair for Arnold, and a fancy upholstered chair of carved wood for Emilie. The highlight of the new apartment was the salon, a reception room with furniture of carved ebony wood. The room contained a settee and armchair, upholstered with the finest damask cloth, and a glass-enclosed hutch that contained precious Meissner figurines and miniature furniture, including a baby grand piano of silver filigree. Later, we grandchildren were allowed, under Emilie's supervision, to play with the miniature furniture. These were considered pieces of art, not toys.

Emilie's third child, a girl, Toni was born in April 1884. She had such a sunny disposition and was so cute that Emilie reconciled herself to having another girl. A family portrait taken that year shows proud, smiling parents, fat baby, and Frieda and Hedwig dressed up as little boys.

In 1887, Emilie was 29 years old and Frieda was already in school when the next girl, my mother Martha, was born. "This is my last try," said Emilie,and handed the girl to a wet nurse. Her disappointment was bitter and Arnold had to bear the brunt of Emilie's complaints. Toni, who was three years old, was delighted with her new, live doll.

While Frieda and Hedwig were in school, the two little girls played blissfully together, unconcerned by the frequent, noisy fights between their parents. They adored their stern and remote father while they resented their ever-nagging mother. Martha and Toni's dolls were alive to them. They created a happy family, with Tony as a just and loving father, and Martha a lenient, easy going mother. The dolls, Alma and Aennchen, were named after a story about live dolls that their nanny had read to them. Alma was the older and more aggressive of the two, and Aennchen was the little dumb sister. There was no limit to their imagination of all the trouble their dolls got into.

This happy family life would be called 'play therapy' today in which they created a happy family atmosphere.

Their idyll was shattered when it was time for Toni to go to school. Without Toni it was no fun to play with Alma and Aennchen. Martha used to flee to the kitchen were the cook consoled her with tidbits and leftovers whenever she appeared with tears in her round, gray eyes. Nobody was concerned that Martha got rounder and rounder. She was such a cute, cuddly child. Only Toni kidded her and began to call her "my little stuffed pigeon." The family continued to travel many summers to Tuchel to visit Arnold's family. While

Emilie dreaded the long voyage and the night in the sleeping car, her daughters were delighted, especially since Arnold was a changed person during those trips, completely devoted to enjoying his daughters. He bought candies and little toys for them, and treated them with unforgettable meals in the dining car.

The numerous Bernhard cousins had grown up and new babies came every year. Their older cousins, Bruno, Danny and Simon Cohn, alternately spoiled and teased them. Frieda was now a teenager and had a crush on her cousin Simon to whom she would later become engaged.

A picture taken around 1900 in the Bernhard's dining room shows the five Bernhard girls with their cousins Bruno and Danny. They are playing family. Danny and Frieda are the parents. Martha and Toni are in a group with their tutor, Bruno. Ada, the baby, carries her doll and Hede is Ada's Nanny. The etagere above the love seat is typical of Emilie's taste for knicknacks.

Toni

Bruno

Danny

Hedwig

Martha

Frieda

Ada

II. Turn Of The Century

For Martha, the beginning of school meant an escape from her prison at home. She easily made friends, and in first grade she had already embarked on her lifelong friendship with Lily Erlanger, a dark-haired girl with a macabre sense of humor. They sat next to each other for eleven school years, and they shared good and bad teachers and much of their free time. However, Lily had no use for childish games and dolls. She liked wilder games, while Toni and Martha continued to live occasionally in their make-believe world with Alma and Aennchen, who went from time to time to the doll doctor and got new clothes every Christmas season.

Frieda was aloof and serious. She grew up to be a stunning beauty with luminous, pale, clear skin, large dark eyes, and shining auburn hair. Her many admirers left her cold. She accepted only her cousin, Simon, as a trusted friend.

Finally, the time came for a visit of the relatives from West Prussia. For weeks, the house was cleaned and shined, curtains and carpets were sent out to be cleaned, windows and glass doors were washed, furniture was polished, and every knickknack was polished or dusted.

When the day of their arrival finally came, Hedwig was in the bedroom wing of the apartment, applying the final touches of hospitality, filling the vases with flowers, setting out fresh towels in the guest rooms, humming a happy tune to herself, while the rest of the family was at the train station waiting to welcome the guests. At last, the doorbell rang. Hedwig, dustcloth in her hand, rushed to the door. The glass door between the two wings of the house was closed, but was invisible in its freshly washed splendor. Hedwig ran right through it, shattering the glass, and cutting her nose in many places.

As the family and guests entered the house, Hedwig lay huddled on the floor, her face and dress, as well as the floor, covered with blood. They carried her to a bed and called the doctor. Hedwig cried and hid her face in a towel that was soon soaked through with blood.

The doctor assured the family that no vital organ was affected, and stitched her nose to the best of his ability. All through the guests' visit, Hedwig had to stay home, her face swathed in bandages. When the bandages were finally removed, Hede's nose was badly scarred and disfigured. The heartbreak of her ugliness was never far from her thoughts. Her fate was sealed from then on. Nobody would ever fall in love with this ugly, clumsy person. While, for onlookers, the scars were nearly invisible; in her imagination they were her most prominent feature. She always remained in the background and, sad to say, her sisters treated her as the ugly duckling who never would ever turn into a swan.

Emilie suffered a great shock in the summer of 1897 when she found out that she was pregnant again at the age of nearly forty. The house reverberated with her desperate accusations against poor Arnold. She alternated between hysterics and passivity, lying on the sofa with an unread book in her hand, brooding and being sorry for herself, demanding silence from everyone.

During this time, her daughters fled the house in despair. Their asylum was the two Ottensooser families. Both Wilhelm and Eugen had lovely young wives, and each of them had two sons at that time. Wilhelm and Eugen had established a modest banking business. Wilhelm had lost his first wife when she gave birth to their son Robert in 1890. Wilhelm did not wait long to give his son a new mother, Martha Herzheimer from Mainz in the Rhineland. She was a girl full of the joy of life for which the Rhine Valley is so famous. Her pretty face smiled easily. Her first baby died, and she gave all her love to her stepson Robert whom she always considered her own child. In 1895 she gave birth to a son, Kurt and the Bernhard girls adored the two little boys, as well as the cheerfulness of the Ottensooser household.

Eugen had also married a lovely rich girl, and they had two sons, Fritz and Ernst. Emilie resented her sisters-in-law for their good looks and cheerfulness, but, most of all she was jealous because they both had sons. She was also jealous because her daughters so obviously preferred their young aunts to her. While Emilie sulked in her darkened living room, the girls went with one or the other of the Ottensooser families on their Sunday outings. Sometimes Arnold joined them. They took the tramway to the end station, walked for half an hour or so to a coffeehouse where the ladies had coffee and cake, and the men drank beer. More often than not, they hired a carriage, or on the Donau Main Canal took the "Schlagrahmdampfer," called the whipped cream steamboat because at the end of the line there was a a restaurant that was famous for its rich desserts topped with whipped cream. Martha continued to rave about the Schlagrahmdampfer into her old age.

Emilie gave birth to her 5th daughter, Ada, in February 1898, when Martha was ten years old. Emilie rejected the baby when they put the whimpering bundle into her arms and handed the child over to the wet nurse who was hired before Ada's birth. Emilie's mother Adelheid had died quietly a few years earlier, so it was natural that the baby was named after her. Martha mothered the new baby from the start, but, when Ada was a toddler, Emilie became plagued by guilt feelings about her early rejection of her youngest child. She developed an unhealthy protectiveness and an irrational fear her frail, delicate girl might get sick and die. She put her to bed at the first sneeze or cough, and when the little girl complained about stomach pains, she put her on a strict diet of gruel and biscuits which in turn made the child even more delicate and frail.

The "Schlajrahm Dampfer." The "Whipped Cream" excursions boat on the Donau—the Main Canal that connects the Atlantic with the Black Sea.

Years passed, and when Frieda was 20 years old, she got engaged to her first love, her cousin Simon Cohn, who had moved to Berlin and was a traveling salesman for ladies' wear. He managed to come to Nuernberg on his business trips, and their romance seemed to blossom.

Emilie left the sofa long enough to go shopping with her oldest daughter to buy a rich and elegant trousseau and a gorgeous wedding gown. Frieda was listless during the shopping sprees and showed little interest. Emilie was so engrossed in the shopping that she barely noticed her daughter's remoteness, and neither her sisters nor Arnold were alarmed. The only one who warned the family that something seemed to be wrong with Frieda was her aunt, Martha Ottensooser. She was only a few years older than Frieda, and was the only person in the family who had close ties to her. She suspected that Emilie had warned her daughter that Simon was too closely related to her, and that her offspring might affected. Emilie was also concerned that Simon was a Prussian, and that she feared the newlyweds would leave Nuernberg to live in Berlin.

Nevertheless, the wedding date was set, and the synagogue and hall were reserved for May 1901. Simon was expected to spend the week before the wedding in Nuernberg. The other guests would arrive later. Frieda was very moody and withdrawn the day before his arrival. She excused herself after dinner to go for a walk.

She was not seen again until she was dragged out of the river the next day, an apparent suicide. Nobody had any explanation for the disaster. Simon was desolate to find his bride dead. Frieda's death cast a deep shadow over the family.

Life went on in the Bernhard household and the daughters grew up to be presented to society. The means of doing this was the "Tanzstunde." The Tanzstunde, lessons in ballroom dancing, were a cherished institution of the upper middle class in Germany since the middle of the 19th century or earlier. A group of 10 to 12 couples took instructions together at a respected dancing school like the Krebs Institute in Nuernberg. Young men between 18 and 20 years of age asked young girls between the ages of 16 and 17 to be their partners, usually upon suggestions by their mothers. This custom was more widely adhered to in our Jewish society than in society at large. Only a few of the Christian girls in our school attended a Tanzstunde, while most of the Jewish girls were invited as partners before the end of their 10th year of school. Instructions began in fall with a few lessons to learn the dance steps, just the girls and boys by themselves, so that the clumsy ones would not be embarrassed. Then came the great event when each boy and each girl was introduced to the parents and their friends. Many months of dancing lessons followed, in which boys and girls danced together to the music of a trio. Each weekly lesson was a social affair with chaperones and a visit to a cafe after the lesson.

Before the final grand ball was another event, the cotillion. During this last dancing lesson in Mr. Kreb's establishment, the young ladies and young men assembled before each dance in their dressing rooms, where they each got a flower made from silk ribbons of different colors, called cotillions. Each boy and girl with the same color of ribbons had to dance together. This music was repeated throughout the evening.

The crowing event of the Tanzstunde was the coming-out ball, a great dance in the largest dance hall of the town with a sit-down dinner, a great band, and a polonaise, during which each couple was introduced. The girls had huge bouquets in their arms, given to them by their admirers, and the size of the bouquet was an indication of the popularity of each girl.

Another popularity contest was the "dance card," a little booklet where each dance was recorded, and the boys wrote their names in a girl's card for the dances they intended to dance with her. It was a matter of honor to have one's dance card filled before the dancing even started.

How do I know all this? Very simple; twenty-five years later it was my turn to have my lessons with Mr. Krebs, and the ritual had not changed except that we did not have "dance-cards," and it was a matter of great confusion to remember to whom each dance was promised. The routine, then as later, was broken from time to time, when a dance was proclaimed a "ladies' choice."

Martha and her sisters collected their cotillions with their dance cards, along with favors and menus of the parties and weddings to which they went in a huge "bottomless" cigar box, which we children loved to explore, and which helped me to piece together my story.

Hede was not popular in her Tanzstunde. Only the brother of her girl friend took her on dates, at the urging of his sister. This young man became Hedwig's only remembrance throughout her life of anything resembling a romance.

While Toni was busy with her Tanzstunden experience, Martha experienced the first great love of her life. She and Lily fell in love with their teacher, Fraulein Koenig, the "Queen."

At that time, Germany had a law that prevented married women from teaching. The idea was that married women could not devote their full attention to their job. Male teachers dominated education, while female teachers were usually dried out old spinsters. It was something very special when a young and beautiful woman like Marthilde Koenig was hired as a teacher of French in the "Hoehere Maedchenschule", the secondary school for girls, which my grandmother, my mother and her sisters, and later I, attended. Koenig means king, koenigin is queen. So Miss Koenig was known all over the school as "die Koenigin", The "Queen." She was not only pretty, but a good teacher, and all her students adored her. Lily however, went overboard with her admiration which was more than just a normal crush on a teacher. Martha, Lily's best friend, participated willingly in the cult of the queen.

All the girls in the school adored their young French teacher, but Martha and Lily outdid them all. Martha and Lily liked to stay after school. They helped Miss Koenig correct papers, carried her books, and walked her home. They spent hours in the street in front of her house in the hope of catching a glimpse of her, a shadow behind drawn curtains. They spent countless hours raving about her.

My first school which was also the school of my mother and aunts.

When their 10th year of school, the year of graduation, grew to a close, Martha and Lily could not stand the thought that this would mean the end of their worship. They convinced the director of their school to add an eleventh year of study as preparation for a teacher's certificate. Lily and Martha were tireless in recruiting students for this class. Even Toni consented to go to school with them.

This last year of school was a time of complete bliss. Never has anybody loved school more than Fraulein Koenig's eleventh grade. Although it was for Martha and Lily the year of their Tanzstunde, its diversions paled compared with their deep devotion to their queen. The young men with whom Martha flirted halfheartedly were mere shadows, and though Arthur Braun, her future husband, was one of her partners, she barely noticed him. Lily did not flirt at all, because she would feel unfaithful to her true love.

At the end of the school year, in spring 1905, Toni, Lily, and Martha went with their classmates and Fraulein Koenig to the county seat in Ansbach to take an examination for a teacher's certificate, though Arnold strongly opposed the idea. But strangely enough, Emilie convinced Arnold to let the girls get their certificate. She said it would be a "nest egg" for them, in case they could not get married. However, Martha and Toni had to promise never to take a paid position as long as they lived with their parents. The days in Ansbach with the beloved queen as chaperone were exasperating and exhilarating, and all three passed with flying colors.

During the following school year they were able to complete their student teaching as assistants of Fraulein Koenig, but after the year was over there was a great void in their lives.

On Martha's 18th birthday, her friend Lily gave her a diary, bound in red leather, with lock and key. While we children were allowed to rummage through the cigar box and Mama's collection of photographs, none of us was ever allowed to open the diary, which also contained love letters from Arthur. When Mama died, we decided that I would open the diary, read it, and then destroy it. Yet, I am going to use some facts from the diary for the next chapters.

Martha, Toni, Ada and Hede in their Sunday finery.

III. The Years Until 1910

During the years of the reign of the "Queen," Martha had neglected her little sister Ada. But Ada had found a new playmate, her cousin Nelly Ottensooser, Martha Ottensooser's daughter who was born in 1899, when Ada was a year old.

A problem arose when Ada had to start school. With Emilie's increasing and obsessive overprotectiveness towards her, Ada missed school very often, because Emilie put her to bed at the least symptom of indisposition. Martha had to tutor her, and Ada clung to her older sister as the only sunshine in her life.

During her adolescence, Martha was wretched. From her diary, it was obvious that Martha was deeply unhappy about her home life, which erupted again and again in wild sessions of shouting, shrieking, and despair. The most insignificant incident could trigger a wild shouting match between the parents, or the girls and their parents, or among the girls themselves. The effect on Martha was prolonged seizures of weeping. In June 1905 she writes in her diary:

"Oh that unholy weeping. I think I have cried today all day long. I pity my poor eyes. I am sure I will repent one day that I have wept so much in my youth. But the more I resolve to conquer this compulsion to weep, as soon as anybody says a cross word to me when I am in this disposition, all self-control is gone. I know that I am dreaming too much, and that reality cannot be as perfect as my dreams, but I am missing heartfelt encouragement, trust, love, or whatever it is. When I weep like that, I find threats and punishment from my father. Mother gets even madder and is angry at me. Toni gives me mockery and contempt. Hedwig reacts with indifference, with malicious pleasure, or even with pity, the same as Ada. Can this help me? On such days I especially endeavor to do my duty, but everything goes wrong. What terrible thing I must have done that God makes me so unhappy.''

After this outburst, Toni wrote in the diary, ''You clumsy, dejected little person. I have read all of it, and in spite of your silly despair, I have read it with great enjoyment.''

After this entry in 1905, Martha did not write again in her diary until December 1908. During those years, Martha played tennis and had lessons in painting with Toni. Some of their sketchbooks still exist, and show skill and promise. They still spent summers in Tuchel, in Danzig, or in Berlin, where some of their cousins had settled. On one of their

Toni and Hans.

visits in Berlin, Toni, who was now 25, and a distant cousin, Hans Ludwig, fell in love and got engaged. Hans was a reporter for a famous Berlin newspaper, and an ardent sportsman. His favorite sport was rowing. Toni did not like to exert herself, but she steered their little rowboat and accompanied him on his outings on the many lakes around Berlin.

Emilie was disappointed that her daughter was going to marry a "Saupreusse," but her objections were drowned out by the joy of the rest of the family. The wedding was a great feast, and right after the wedding Toni left to set up her new household in Berlin.

Between 1905 and 1910, most of Martha's classmates got married. But Martha and Lily gave little thought to marriage and courtship. Lily's parents, rich merchants in hops, were concerned about their headstrong daughter, who never showed interest in men, and invited as a "housefriend" a young man, Oscar Bruckmann, who was just starting his career by buying hops from the farmers. Nuernberg was the center of the hops market, an indispensable commodity in beer-drinking Bavaria, and the hops market was dominated by Jews who were speculators, many of whom became very rich. The business was concentrated in the hands of a few families, and Oscar was eager to marry into one of those families like the Erlangers, especially since Lily would have a considerable dowry.

When he proposed, Lily accepted him because she was tired of the prodding by her parents. Later, after her wedding night, Lily confided to Martha that Oscar had done terrible things to her and she would never again sleep with him in the same bed. A son was born to her in due time, but he remained an only child, whose parents had separate bedrooms.

While Martha was in a stage of sexual awakening, Toni invited her for a prolonged stay in Berlin. She left Nuernberg in May of 1910 and arrived in Berlin after a pleasant train journey, where a pregnant Toni and a beaming Hans awaited her to take a taxi to their cozy home in Friedenau.

During the years before World War I, Berlin was the most exciting city in Germany, maybe in all of Europe. The capitals of Europe were old and well established, while Berlin was the youngest capital. It was famous for its huge parks, the broad, tree-lined avenues, its grandiose buildings, theaters, museums, hotels, restaurants, elegant department stores, pretentious palaces, and government buildings. Most of Berlin was built in the nineteenth century in a mixture of a neoclassical and neo-Gothic style, an architectural mishmash that was frowned upon by purist art critics. But, ugly or not, the city was alive with ideas, enthusiasm, prosperity, and artistic experiments.

Martha came from a town with a rich cultural past, of a quaint but faded beauty, but provincial compared with the capital. For the first time in her life she experienced the excitement of a metropolis. It was the end of the theater season, but she was able to attend many performances of operas, plays and concerts. The operas of Richard Strauss were the sensation of the season, and Martha never forgot the spirited performance of the "Rosencavalier" that she attended with Toni and Hans.

She also saw the newest plays of Hofmannsthal and Schnitzler, and saw paintings by the German impressionists Max Liebermann and Lovis Corinth.

Sometimes, Martha took the streetcars from one to the other end of the line. During such rides she got also a glimpse of the backside of the city, row after row of dark dreary tenements in treeless, dirty streets, where the working masses had to live in a world apart from the luxury and the prosperity of the elegant facade of the city. These dreary streets were the breeding ground of the socialist party of Germany.

The following episode is not mentioned in Martha's diary,

but when I once asked her whether she had kissed any man before her marriage, she said that she was kissed by Toni's brother-in-law during her stay in Berlin. That was all I knew about the incident until, in her old age, when she liked to talk freely about sex, she said, "I never told you what happened between Leo and me. This is how it was..."

"I once stayed overnight in Anna's house. Her husband Leo was a budding architect of the school of Art Nouveau of Jugendstill as it was called in Germany. In the middle of the night, the door opened and Leo entered the room in his nightshirt. He kissed me tenderly and sat down on my bed. He said, 'Please let me lie down beside you. Nothing will happen to you.' That was all but it upset me so much that I thought a lot about it. You are the first person to whom I told the real story."

Later when I was the same age as my mother had been at the time of this incident, I had dinner at Anna's house while visiting the Ludwigs. After dinner, Leo got a sketchbook and made numerous sketches of me and said, 'Give these to your mother from me. You look just as she looked when she was your age.'

After Martha's return to Nuernberg, a young man called at her house and wanted to talk to her. This young man was Arthur Braun.

Drawing by Leo.

IV. Arthur Braun

Arthur was a "Landjude," a Jew who grew up in a little town where Jews lived a modest life as small shopkeepers, merchants, craftsmen, and occasionally farmers, who had limited educational opportunities, and kept Jewish law and traditions. Many of their children resented the narrow confines of small town life, and moved to larger cities, as the Ottensoosers and Bernhards had done one generation earlier.

In the cities, well-established city Jews who had become wealthy and who had acquired social graces, looked down upon these country bumpkins, forgetting their own small-town roots.

Arthur's parents traded in animal skins and furs, as did most of their relatives in the little town of Niederstetten in the Duchy of Wuertemberg. Besides the fur business, Arthur's father, Wolf Braun, had a tavern and cafe, which was the center of Jewish social life in town. In his book about the Jews of Niederstetten, the author Bruno Stern mentions the Braun's cafe on many occasions when the whole Jewish congregation went there after the Sabbath services or on Jewish holidays.

Wolf and Sarah Braun had ten children, but only six of them survived to adulthood, my uncles Issi, Adolf and Simon, my aunts Babette Rosenfelder and Hannchen Gans, and my father Arthur.

Arthur and his brothers visited the local Realschule, that required tuition, a secondary school that taught French and math in addition to the subjects taught in the free public school. However, this school ended with the seventh grade, and only a few of the young people continued to study in a nearby larger town, Bad Mergentheim. The sons of Wolf

Braun were not among them. The two girls, Babette and Hannchen, however, were sent to a cooking and home economics school for young Jewish girls, in the resort town Bad Mergentheim, which was connected with a large, Jewish-owned hotel.

My father, in contrast to my mother and grandmother, told us very little about his childhood. It seems that he was embarrassed and ashamed by his incomplete education and did not want to be reminded of it.

I recall him telling only two stories from his childhood. One story he liked to tell was of the time when he stole apples, was chased by the owner of the orchard, fell down from the tree and suffered a big hole in his head.

Another story that he told and retold was the following incident: one day, the boys of the public school ganged up to prevent his little brother Simon from going to school. Simon ran crying home, where he found Arthur, whom he told his plight. Arthur went back with him and beat up the boys so that they fled. Arthur was a hero thereafter, and especially Simon adored and admired him for the rest of his life.

By the time Arthur left school, his older brothers Issi and Adolf had left home to settle in Nuernberg, along with their older sister Hannchen who went with them to keep house. With the blessing of their parents, and whatever money they could give them, they opened a small furniture store.

Arthur had to stay home to help his parents with the business. He traded throughout the countryside in a one-horse carriage to buy hides from the farmers. He carried large amounts of money to pay for the hides. On his trips, he used to sleep in small country inns. He hid the money at night under his pillow, and could barely sleep for fear that robbers and thieves were after him. He retained an irrational fear of thieves throughout his life. When people made fun of him because he went to check the locks and windows every evening, he always told about his lonely trips and his fear. Arthur was also very ambitious. He improved his education by extended reading and, finally, he left his hometown to join his brothers in Nuernberg. According to him, it was he who turned a small, sleazy operation into a flourishing furniture business.

He was an energetic young man, good looking, with an unending thirst for knowledge and education. He found a non-Jewish friend whose name was Zuern who was a furniture designer with bold, new ideas. He was a lover of art, and taught Arthur the history of art and drawing. Zuern, his young wife, and two lovely blonde daughters lived next door to Arthur's sister.

Arthur was also interested in being a member of the higher Jewish society in Nuernberg. As a means to this end, Hannchen suggested that he should join one of Mr. Krebs' dancing classes. Arthur was a lady's man and flirted with all the young girls in this group which included my mother. He liked Martha, and even sent her postcards from his frequent business trips. I was amused when I found some of them in my mother's collection of postcards. They showed sentimental pictures of pretty girls, and were addressed to Fraulein Bernhard, and he addressed her with the formal "Sie" rather than the familiar "du." Martha had other beaus, but made special mention in her diary that she received postcards from Arthur Braun.

Arthur enjoyed the life of an unhampered bachelor for several years until his business needed an infusion of money. At that time, Hannchen advised him to go to a matchmaker and marry a girl with a dowry. Arthur obediently obliged. But none of the matchmaker's prospects appealed to him. Furthermore, he believed in love, not matchmaking, as the basis of a happy marriage. He left the matchmaker, who made a last suggestion. "They are not my clients, but the Bernhards have a nice daughter. However, she has only a modest dowry."

When girls of the working class got married, their only responsibility to their future husbands was to contribute a trousseau, consisting of bedding, bed sheets, tableware and other articles for the household, but the father of middle and upper class girls was expected to pay the future husband an agreed upon sum of money to enable him to take care of his daughter. The sum of money depended upon the financial status of the family. This dowry was in addition to the trousseau which the bride (or her family) was expected to contribute. Since Arnold was not a rich man, and had five daughters, Toni and Martha's dowries were modest compared, for instance, to Lily's dowry whose parents were wealthier.

When Martha got married, she compared her own and Toni's trousseau in a little notebook, because she insisted on getting the same value as her sister.

The remembrance of the pretty, chubby girl came as a lightening bolt to Arthur. "That's the one," he said, and immediately went to the Bernhards to propose. Martha promptly and irrevocably fell deeply in love with him. The postcards from his business trips continued. Suddenly the tone changed to "My dear Martha," and the pictures on the postcards were from the places he visited -- no more pretty girls.

They were engaged in November of 1910 and a radiant Martha married him on March 5, 1911.

Martha Bernhard and Arthur Braun,
the engaged couple.

V. The Newlyweds

The night before the wedding, Martha had to sleep in a spare room because her room was given to Toni, Hans, and their baby daughter, Elfriede who came from Berlin. As she was ready to go to bed, an army of cockroaches marched out from under the dresser. Martha was terrified and spent the night sitting on her bed, thinking of her sad childhood and the wonderful future that awaited her, but without giving much thought about the adventure of her wedding night, which was unknown territory for her. Nobody had ever prepared her for it, except Lily with her horror story, which she believed only halfheartedly.

She was extremely tired the next, strenuous day. A civil ceremony at city hall was prescribed by law and was usually later followed by a religious ceremony. It was a clear, nippy Sunday morning when they set out in a horse-drawn taxi to the civil registry, but when they arrived it was closed because it was Sunday. They were told that one was open in the suburbs, and they had a pleasant drive in the country, but Martha nodded and had a nap on Arthur's shoulder because of her sleepless night.

The religious wedding ceremony took place in the elaborate synagogue which had become a famous landmark in Nuernberg, built in Moorish style and lavishly decorated, extraordinarily ambitious for a congregation that consisted of only two percent of the city's population. It was later destroyed by the Nazis.

After the ceremony, more than 50 guests drove to a fashionable ballroom, where they had a sit-down dinner, interrupted by many toasts, and the reading of the "Hochzeitszeitung," their wedding newspaper. It was printed in the format of a regular newspaper, and contained

Rear view of the Synagogue from the Pegnitz.

articles that dealt in a humorous way with incidents in the lives of family members. The lead article was a description of Arthur's escapade with his friend Zuern. Both of them had been bar-hopping during the night, and in the early morning hours they staggered through the silent streets, singing at the top of their voices until they were arrested by the police for disturbing the peace. Other articles and ads were about every member of the family, with jokes and puns. During a lull, Toni's baby Elfriede also let herself be heard, with a loud tribute that nobody could understand. We often amused ourselves reading this and others of the many Hochzeitszeitungen, and continued the tradition when we got married. Martha collected these papers in her huge cigar box.

The menu, which we also found in the bottomless cigar box, consisted of assorted hors d'oeuvres, soup, fish, three entrees of meat and fowl with vegetables and salads, each course accompanied by a suitable wine, followed by coffee, tortes, ice cream, cheeses, and champagne.

Soon after the guests had finished the banquet, an additional crowd of friends of the newlyweds arrived for the evening's entertainment. A lavish, cold buffet was set out, casks of beer flowed endlessly, and between the dances Martha's and Arthur's friends and cousins performed skits or recited poems that they had composed for the occasion.

The cigar box contained copies of a poem by Ada about their childhood, skits by Lily and other school friends of Martha's, poems by the young Ottensooser cousins, and lastly a poem by Zuern that ended with the words "In December we will see each other again."

Martha and Arthur escaped before the dancing was over. They stayed overnight in the Grand Hotel, with the wedding unconsummated because Martha fell asleep as soon as her head hit the pillow. They left early the next morning for a trip to Italy where they rested for a week at Lake Garda, and spent another week in Venice. What can be said about their honeymoon? It is well documented with postcards, menus, and travel folders in the bottomless cigar box. They were deeply in love, and for Martha it was the first time in her life that she was blissfully happy and carefree.

When they returned from their honeymoon, they rented a small apartment not far from the business in the Fuertherstrasse that they furnished modestly and where they had barely enough room for Martha's trousseau.

Arthur got the first jolt in his marital bliss when Martha declared that she did not want to cook for them, but insisted on hiring a maid who could also cook. Arthur had looked forward to eating food cooked by his wife. He was tired of restaurants and food indifferently prepared by paid help.

Both his sisters-in-law and his sister Hannchen were good cooks and prepared the family dinners themselves.

Martha enjoyed her first year of marriage, meeting her friends, going shopping with Lily, visiting parents and relatives, or just sitting in an armchair. She became pregnant immediately and the pregnancy was an easy one. Because Emilie's habit of lying on the sofa was so distasteful to her children, Martha never lay down on the sofa. Instead, she indulged her laziness by sitting in an armchair; however, she got inordinately fat, reading and munching candies.

Many of her former schoolfriends were also pregnant. Lily's son Heinz was born less than a year before me. Toni had her second daughter Elvira six weeks before I was born. Emilie, mother of so many girls, was disappointed when Martha produced another daughter in December, as Zuern had predicted at the wedding. But Martha's and Arthur's joy was unbounded. Martha wrote in her diary that just as she could not understand during her adolescence why she was so unhappy, now she could not understand why so much happiness was showered upon her.

She writes, "No use to ponder about the why, but accept with gratitude. And be thankful, not to a personal God, but to life itself. All that I dreamed about in my wildest dreams has come true. I have a husband who loves me deeply, and whom I love with every fiber of my heart, who has given me the sweetest of babies, our Steffi."

Her only source of concern was the continued unhappiness in her parents' house, with Hedwig and Ada suffering under the violent temper outbursts and hysterics of their mother. Martha wrote that she still suffered from her compulsion to weep, mostly after a visit to her former home, but she hoped that Arthur would help her to overcome this weakness.

While Martha still turned to God in her adolescent days, in 1912 she is thankful to life itself, not to a personal God. This

Mama Martha and baby Steffi.

reflects Arthur's philosophy, in which he rejected formalized religion and believed that only narrow-minded people needed the consolation of religious services and prayer.

Shortly before my birth, Martha and Arthur moved to a large apartment on the same block as his two brothers, Issi and Adolph. Adolph's wife, Meta, nee Goldschmidt, came from a wealthy family and was a model housewife. She was dark, well proportioned, with good features but little brains. When I was born, her youngest daughter was already five years old and their two sons were in school. Issi's first wife died in childbirth after her third child, Martha, was born. He was anxious to find a mother for his children, but his oldest son, Julius, was severely retarded. Luckily, he found an ideal wife in Ida Oestreicher, who came from a family with many retarded members, who was resigned to have no children of her own because she was afraid to have a retarded child. She was overjoyed to marry a widower with children. If there was ever a case to refute the story of the bad stepmother, Ida was the model. She not only gave love and mothering to Alex and Martha, the normal children, but she showered love upon her poor idiot son, whom she adored.

Under her tutorship, Julius, or Lulu, as he called himself, learned to speak and to take care of his personal needs. She was the proudest of mothers when he made a little progress or recognized members of the family. When he met Martha for the first time, he gave her the name Atubaut (Arthur's bride), a fact about which Ida liked to boast. I was afraid of Lulu when I was a child, but he was quite harmless. He played with marbles, or looked out of the second floor window. He knew a lot of people, and greeted them as he recognized them, when they were passing by. Later, when he grew older, Ida gave him a collection of postcards with pictures of pretty girls. He looked at the pictures again and again, kissed them, and relieved his sexual tensions while fondling them.

Arthur and Martha's apartment was furnished with furniture models from the store, a dining room of golden birch wood, a salon of red mahogany wood and wonderful upholstered armchairs, a living room of oak with a corner buffet, inlaid with ebony wood, a sofa flanked by two small book cases, a little sewing table for Martha in front of the window, and a piano that Martha never used except to play children's songs for us, a bedroom in dark mahogany wood that would finally end up in the house of Jacob's sister in Jerusalem, a spare room with custom-built wardrobes for Martha's ample trousseau, and a bed for houseguests, a large kitchen, and a tiny cubbyhole off the kitchen for the cook and the maid.

Arthur liked to bring customers to show them his model home, and, to Martha's despair, sold the salon furniture she

loved so much to one of them. Afterward, the room was furnished as a "Herrenzimmer," a room for the man of the
house, in dark walnut consisting of a large bookcase, an even
larger desk, various armchairs, and a small table. Martha got
reconciled to the new furniture because she loved to buy
books, and soon filled the bookcase to overflowing with an
encyclopedia, works of art, and a collection of German and
international classics, an interminable source of reading and
education for us children. She later carried all her books with
her to Jerusalem, and now we don't know what to do with
them because the new generation does not read German any
more.

Emilie, Arnold and baby Steffi.

On December 14, 1911, Martha gave birth to me at home with the help of a doctor and the only Jewish midwife in Nuernberg, Frau Metzger. The fact that I was a girl was a bitter disappointment for my grandmother Emilie. Martha was expected to nurse her daughter, but the milk flowed only sparsely. Martha obliged everyone's advice, and drank malt beer that was supposed to stimulate milk production and which she hated, and consumed soups which she also disliked, but no milk was produced, and little Steffi wailed hungrily. A wet nurse was hired and, ever after, Martha never ate soups or drank malt beer.

The household was now quite large because, besides a wet nurse, Steffi had a baby nurse, and both were living in. Within a few weeks, all kinds of things were disappearing, until it was discovered that the wet nurse had pilfered them. She was summarily dismissed, and Steffi was put on a formula which resulted in diarrhea and endless whimpering and loss of weight until a new wet nurse was found. Again, peace reigned in the Braun household, but not for long. After a period of growth, Steffi lost weight again and cried for hours on end. The wet nurse had run dry. By that time the baby could be weaned, and henceforth ate and ate to her heart's content until she was rosy, round, and fat like a little pig. In a photo taken when she was one year old, she was nearly as wide as she was tall.

Martha got pregnant again, and gave birth to a stillborn baby, a boy that had strangled on the umbilical cord. As Lily put it, he had committed suicide in his mother's womb. It was the first male in the Bernhard family. Emilie was more heartbroken than the parents who knew they could have other children.

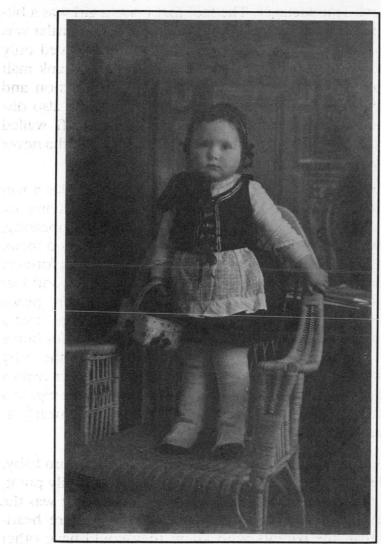

Steffi.

VI. World War I

On December 27, 1913, Martha wrote in her diary: "...so much has happened since I wrote last, but all is still the same. We love each other so strongly and deeply. This must be forever. Thus it is easy to go through hard times when you have such a treasure. The miscarriage in May was bad enough, but I am again with child. Only, if the little boy for whom we hope will be another miscarriage, I will remember it with sorrow. Our little Steffi, who gives us so much happiness, may she always be healthy and develop as well as she does now. Health is the main thing. If I only did not have that gloomy foreboding that attacks me in the middle of greatest merriment..."

Toni gave birth to another daughter, Irene, in February 1914. Emilie was quite despondent. Although she was only in her fifties, she played the invalid, and stayed most of the day lying on her sofa. She believed that she had given the curse of her own life, the curse of not having sons, to her own daughters. When the time came for my mother to give birth, nobody was interested, because war against Russia and France had been declared, and general mobilization held the nation in turmoil. On August 4, 1914, England also declared war against Germany, because Germany had invaded neutral Belgium on its way to invade France. Flags were waving from every house. Germany was in a frenzy of war fever. Everybody was expecting an easy victory. Patriotism was at its height, and old and young men eagerly enlisted as volunteers.

My father was at the recruiting office to volunteer for the army when Mama's labor started, but, fortunately, they could not use Arthur Braun because he had an open cyst on his neck. He later served in the citizen's defense which was a group of rejects from the regular army who learned to use weapons to help defend the country in case of an invasion. With Martha were Emilie, the old family doctor, and the midwife, Mrs. Metzger, when the great event took place. A grandson was born to her, Emilie.

She later told me that this was the happiest day in her life. She was a new person after this, her aches and pains forgotten. She devoted the rest of her life to the task of grandmothering with such zest and success that Lily used to say to my mother, "Your mother should have been born as a grandmother."

I dimly remember the day Wolfgang was born. Our maid showed me a feather on the windowsill and said it was from the angel who had brought my little brother. I also remember kissing my mother who was in bed with the tiny baby.

The second recollection of my life is quite vivid. It was a trip to Berlin. My parents had decided quite suddenly and unexpectedly that they wanted to take a trip to Berlin to visit Toni, before Hans went to war as a medical orderly.

I was taken out of my bed in the middle of the night, and put on the living room table to be dressed. I still can see the gas lamp over my head. It is the only time that I remember having seen gas light because it was soon replaced by electricity. I also remember that we went to the train station in a taxi. When I woke up again, I was with my mother in the lower berth of a sleeping car. I left her and climbed a little ladder to be with my father in the upper berth. When I was dressed, I went into the passageway of the coach, and admired a general in his gray uniform with numerous medals on his chest and an enormous moustache.

The following anecdote is told in the family but I don't remember it. The visit was a complete surprise, and to make it even more so, my parents stayed downstairs and sent me to the second floor to ring the bell. They relished in anticipation the astonished faces of the Ludwig family when they found me standing alone in front of the door. It happened that my

Elfriede, Elvira, Steffi.

cousin Elvira, whom I knew from the previous summer, opened the door and said, "Hi, Steffi. Come, let us play," as if it was the most natural thing in the world that I had come to visit her.

My next recollections are victories and more victories. Flags were fluttering from all the houses and little flags were put on top of the streetcars. I remember marching soldiers, and military bands. As the years passed, the victory celebrations grew fewer and fewer. A gray gloom settled over the land. Martha wrote in her diary in October 1914, when the country was still in its ecstasy of euphoric hope, that she felt she had to write to share her impressions of this great time, now, not later in retrospect.

"We have war. It is not a fairy tale, as unrealistic as it appears to me. We, our generation, are experiencing a war as terrible as the world has ever seen.   For three months we have been in a frenzy. The misery in the world is unimaginable. I cannot describe what unbelieving horror I felt towards war, and still feel. Fortunately, we are far from the front. Today we have witnessed the disaster of war, when Lothar came home wounded. I am asking myself, how is it possible in our refined culture that such a cruel war can be reality? They say that war is a necessity of culture. Is it possible to believe such nonsense? Can this be true? I see only a regression of culture. The men who go to war will become brutal, that is inevitable. And what about health? Those coming back from war will all be damaged. What about the next generation? (I hate to write all this, it sounds as if I wrote a theme for my German class about my thoughts about war.) But I have pondered a hundred times about the war, and felt deeply. That's enough about war.''

Martha then continued to write about her deep love for Arthur, whom she admired, but personal life paled compared with the all encompassing reality of war. As I now read my mother's diary, I am amazed that she had the courage to condemn war in the environment of patriotism and enthusiasm that prevailed during the first year of the war.

However, even I, a small child at the time, remember the war years in a fog of gray. Gray were the uniforms of the soldiers in the street, many of them on crutches, with an empty trouser leg or sleeve where a leg or an arm should have been. Gray was the bread that we ate, gray was the sky, and gray were the faces of our loved ones. I remember autos with three wheels instead of four, to save on tires. I remember the wedding of our maid, in a black wedding dress because a loved one had been killed shortly before. More and more people wore black as a sign of mourning. Uncomprehending, I saw tears in many eyes, and even grandmother had lost her newly found cheer.

I liked to go to her house because she used to bake cookies for us, war cookies that were made of gray flour, a little sugar, water, baking powder, and little else. But they were rolled out with a rolling pin and cut into diamonds which were called "grenade splinters." They looked nice, and we were not accustomed to eating sweets very often.

Our parents tried to protect us from the depressing atmosphere of the war torn city, and bought a lovely villa in a small commuter colony, a half an hour train ride from Nuernberg. Our little house stood halfway up on a hill and was surrounded on three sides by dense forest. The house on the Ludwigshoehe became the paradise of our childhood.

For the first years we lived in the country during summer, and spent the winter in the apartment in Nuernberg. My little brother Heinz was born in 1917 in Nuernberg. At the end of the war, the housing shortage was so great that the government ruled that a family could only have one home, and luckily our parents decided to winterize the villa with central heating and an enclosure of a veranda as additional playroom for us children. In 1918, we finally stayed all year long in the Ludwigshoehe.

During the last winter in Nuernberg when I was 6, an incident occurred that influenced my future life, and filled me with remorse and guilt. The maid had put little Heinz on his potty in his bed while I was quietly playing in the room. I began to tease the baby and he fell in his bed, spilling the mess all over himself and the bed. He yelled, and the maid came running. When she saw the disaster, without delay she gave Heinz a cruel spanking. Heinz shrieked at the top of his voice. Every shriek seared into my soul. I was aware that it was I who should have been spanked, yet I kept silent. I never had felt so miserable in my life before. I could not sleep for several nights, and made a firm resolve that this should never happen again. From now on, I would confess every evil deed I had done, and never let somebody else get punished for my misdeeds. I developed a compulsion to confess every little aberration before it was even discovered, and took my punishment, even if whatever I had done would never be discovered.

Our villa was an oasis of happiness and sunshine during the gloom of war. It was also the target for the Sunday invasion of numerous uncles, aunts, and cousins who came on the train from Nuernberg early in the afternoon, walked dutifully in the forest, and came to our garden for afternoon coffee and cake. Maria, our cook, lamented loudly, but every weekend she produced something like a cake with whatever ingredients were available, brewed coffee out of malt and chicory, and braced herself for the locust invasion of guests who sat under the trees in the garden, and left mountains of unwashed dishes behind.

Some of our neighbors were Jews, and we were in and out of their houses, especially our next-door neighbors', the Wurzinger family. Their son Stephan was my aunt Ada's boyfriend. We had no social contact with the non-Jews in our neighborhood until I went to school with Heini Bollendorf, who became my first boyfriend and who had flaming red hair like mine.

Next to our house, the last in the small colony, were meadows, fields, and the forest. The forest was like an extension of our house, and we spent much of our time picking mushrooms and berries, balancing on fallen trees, dreaming in a hunter's perch high in the trees, following murmuring brooks, and watching fawns, hares, and salamanders. Although my brother and I were still preschoolers, Mama let us roam the forest on our own, as long as we took our dog Fritz along.

Fritz was our unforgettable companion. He was really a person who could not talk, not a dog. He was a highly trained, intelligent Doberman pinscher who had served in the army but was shellshocked, received an honorable discharge as a disabled veteran, and was sold. My parents became the owners of this faithful, fierce, and loyal creature. His only fault was that he became neurotic as soon as he heard a loud noise that reminded him of the war. He spent thunderstorms howling and yapping under a bed or sofa, trembling from head to tail.

Mama brushed him every day, and his fur was shining, his head was held high, and his shortened tail could wag with the deep-felt emotion of true love. He was a wonderful, belligerent watchdog who attacked every intruder, and Mama had to pay for many torn trousers. However, he was trained to bite only into cloth, never into flesh.

During the summer of 1916, Wolfgang and I got violently sick with dysentery. I had a dramatic, high fever. I remember that I was wrapped in cold wet sheets to bring the fever down, and was shrieking at the top of my voice. But after lingering for a few hours at death's doorstep, I recovered quickly and completely. Wolfgang had a slow form of it, with low fever for months on end. He could not digest his food properly, and as a result of the malnutrition he got rickets. His growth was stunted and as a result he remained the smallest child in his class throughout his school life.

When we later learned how to spell, we used to pronounce every word backwards, especially all names. I became Iffets, and Wolfgang was Gnagflow. "Floh" is the German word for flea, and since he was so tiny, the name stuck to him, and he remained Floh for the rest of his life.

After Heinz was born, Mama said that her family was now complete and she did not want another child. She had found a new passion that she shared with her best friend Lily. They both fell in love with movies, and went several times a week to a show, frequenting every moviehouse in town. These

Floh and Steffi.

were the times when movies had subtitles and were in the nickelodeon stage. She also met weekly with her former schoolmates for a kaffeeklatsch. The household was efficiently run by a maid and a cook, with the help of an additional woman who came to the house for laundry and heavy housecleaning. Shopping and making the daily menu were the only household chores performed by Mama.

Young peasant girls went into service as maids or cooks for a few years to collect a trousseau before getting married. My mother usually married her domestic servants off from our house. Grandmother Emilie never had a maid who married. They all left her after a short while because they could not stand her. It was Hedwig who had to help out between changes.

Mama's youngest sister Ada spent the summer of 1917 with us in the "House in the Sun" as she called it. She was a beautiful, delicate, nineteen year old girl, a hot-house plant with clear, luminous skin, large gray eyes and an abundance of shining honey-colored hair that framed her small, pale face. She suffered from stomach ulcers, and often stayed in bed. Her illness was probably the result of her mother's regime to starve her on gruel, zwieback and weak tea as soon as she showed signs of indigestion, which became more and more frequent as she grew older because Ada was the victim of her mother's temper outbursts and wild fights with her husband. War rationing also added to Ada's malnutrition. While she was in our house, my mother and the cook competed with each other to procure little extra treats for her, like eggs, jam, or chicken. I watched with envy, when Ada ate white bread and soft boiled eggs for breakfast, while the rest of us ate black bread with margarine.

Because of her frequent absences from school, Ada was only an average student, but showed promise in music and art. After finishing school, she received instruction in art and

Aunt Ada.

playing the guitar. But she did not have the stamina to become really creative and developed an inferiority complex.

She did not participate in a tanzstunde like her sisters because all the young men were fighting in France or on the Russian front. Most of the unmarried women and young girls did volunteer work. Ada was too frail for this work. She envied her sister Hedwig who worked for the Red Cross in the railway station where she served coffee and snacks to the soldiers who passed through Nuernberg on their way to or from the front.

Ada sat sadly at home and wrote letters to all the young soldiers she knew. Often enough, she got romantically involved with her pen friends and more often than not, they died on the field of honor.

Her generation were the young men who volunteered or who had been drafted into the army as soon as they left school. They were barely trained before they were sent to war as canon fodder. This group had the highest mortality rate in the whole army and left a gap of eligible men that affected a whole generation of women.

Shortly before she came to live with us, three or four of her friends were killed and it was a sad Ada that moved into our attic, where she lived in a small room with slanting walls, two beds, a closet, a desk and two chairs.

She shared this modest abode for seven weeks with her cousin Trude Kuttner, one of the many cousins of her father's family in West Prussia, who became her friend during the visits to Tuchel. They were the same age. Trude, with her sunny disposition, was like medicine for brooding Ada, and the two young girls giggled and whispered together all day long. Wonder of wonders, they even each had a boyfriend. Ada fell in love with Stephan, the son of our Jewish neighbors, who was at home recovering from a minor wound he had sustained. Trude fell in love with Stephan's cousin Hans Leurer who was excused from serving in the army because he had a crippled right hand and who also spent the summer in the Ludwigshoehe. Both cousins intended to study medicine and were close friends. This foursome liked to go on long walks in the forest. Ada usually brought her guitar, and their voices blended beautifully in harmony as they sang German folksongs and lovesongs. As often as I could, I tagged along behind them, listening to their conversations, of which I understood very little, and to their songs. It seemed that the sun shone brighter, the birds sang lovelier and the flowers bloomed more brightly during that long summer of 1917 when finally the Russian army gave up the fight, and new hope filled every heart.

More visitors than ever made the Sunday pilgrimage to our hospitable house and garden. There were all Ada's young girlfriends who were as music loving and artistically gifted as Ada; in addition, there were all of Arthur's and Martha's friends and relatives. Only one sour note entered the bliss of the young people -- when Ada's cousin Nelly Ottensooser also fell in love with Hans, the student of medicine.

As the summer came to a close, Ada returned to her parents, Stephan and Hans Leurer went to the University of Wurzburg and Nelly, who had just passed her abitur and was the first modern girl of the family to attend the university, followed them to Wurzberg to study mathematics.

Ada had a lovely, imaginative mind and used to tell me stories and fairy tales. I remember one that she made up herself. It was the story of the blue forest. The blue forest always beckoned to her near the horizon, and she wanted to go there. So she wandered long and far, and suffered from heat and cold, from hunger and thirst. She walked and walked until her feet were bleeding. But, wherever she went, the forest was green, and far away the blue forest loomed and called, "Come to me, come to me."

Floh, Steffi and Fritz in the forest.

Aunt Ada played with me, pushing the swing far into the sky, where I was free as a bird, or dressing up my little black cat Peter in doll's clothes before I pushed him around in my doll's perambulator. We went together for walks in the green forest, inhabited by princes and princesses who were changed into frogs and salamanders by the bad witch.

Early in 1918, Ada went to the city of Thorn in West Prussia to visit her cousin Trude. They both were busy with volunteer work, entertaining soldiers. Trude played the piano and Ada sang to her guitar accompaniment, and both reaped much applause from their audience. By 1918 it was a bedraggled army, not the enthusiastic self-assured young men of previous years. Though Russia had given up fighting, the war continued on the Western Front. The soldiers who passed through town were the remnants of the fighters on the Eastern Front who were transported to the Western Front. Revolution and strife tore Germany apart internally. Deserters roamed the countryside. I remember that, during the summer of 1918, Mama did not let us roam freely in the forest, even with Fritz's protection.

In the meantime, we moved finally to the Ludwigshoehe. Although Mama said after Heinz' birth that the family was now complete, she got pregnant again. Her irreverent friend Lily called the embryo "the burst condom." Mama got rounder and rounder. We knew that this was because our new little sister Lorle was growing in her belly. One day I drew a footstool near Mama, got on it, and asked her to open her mouth.

"What do you want from me?" she asked crossly.

"I want to tell Lorle to come out soon."

In June, when the strawberries were ready to be picked and the garden was full of roses, Mrs. Metzger, the midwife, was called to spend the last days with us. She enjoyed her vacation, and ate so many strawberries that I was afraid none would be left for us. But, finally, she was busy with Mama. We were not allowed to go to her bedroom. The doctor was called from the nearby town, and, instead of Lorle, our little brother Werner was born.

Nobody took much notice of him. He slept all day on the balcony on the second floor. At first he had a wet nurse, but she was such a disagreeable woman that the house reverberated with her shouting and shrieking. She was soon dismissed, and Marie had to feed him a formula. She also changed his diapers from time to time, but his little behind was red and sore from lack of care. From time to time, one of our visitors climbed the stairs to look at the new baby. Otherwise, the birds in the trees were his only company. To get milk for the baby we had a goat.

Food was quite scarce, and, in order to get well fed, we rented a field where we grew potatoes. We also had rabbits. Whenever a rabbit was eaten, it was disguised as chicken to spare us children the misery of eating one of our pets. But we knew that we had eaten rabbits at some time because our winter coats were trimmed with rabbit fur.

In 1918, we children enjoyed the first winter in the country. We went sledding as soon as there was snow on the ground. We could sled all the way downhill to the train station, and pull the sled back to the top of the hill, from where we had a long, fast slide through the forest. Ada who was in Nuernberg with her parents, fell into a deep depression after her friends were gone. She was sent to a psychiatric clinic because of her depression. Once Ada's group of non-Jewish friends came for a visit on the sixth of December, the feast of St. Ruprecht, the German Santa Claus who visits German children on that day with a switch and a sack with apples, nuts and other goodies. The good children got the goodies, the bad children got the switch. St. Ruprecht came to us that day. My mother said that I had not always been good, and I got threatened with being taken away in St. Ruprecht's huge sack to the forest, where I would learn under a strict regime to be good. I cried, and promised to be better next year, and finally was allowed to take part in the bounty of goodies that were emptied from the sack on the floor.

I wondered why St. Ruprecht would visit Jewish children, until, shortly after, it dawned on me that it was one of our visitors who had dressed up as St. Ruprecht.

Mama stole away as often as she could to spend a day in the city with Lily. They started the festivities with a gourmet lunch, and then they went to one or two movies. They called their outings "Junmgferntag," a spinster day, because they were as carefree and happy as they had been before their marriages.

During her summers in our house, Ada wrote a little volume called "Of Steffi and Wolfgang," in which she wrote incidents and anecdotes about us. The little stories show her whimsical style and tender understanding. Unfortunately, most of the anecdotes are based on puns and children's language, and cannot be translated. However, the booklet helps us to remember funny and significant incidents from our childhood.

One story goes far back to when I was very little. My father had given me a sound spanking, and I was crying at the top of my voice. Suddenly, I stopped and said in a completely normal voice, "I would like to yell much more, but my throat is hurting," and shut up. Often she wrote about my insatiable craving for sweets, and my constant begging for them. Once I watched my aunt eat her breakfast, consisting of her diet of white bread, eggs, and jam, all things unobtainable for us simple mortals who were healthy enough to digest our wartime fare. I looked at her with big round eyes and said, "I really don't want to beg, but, oh, would I like to taste your good food."

The house on Ludwigshohe.

VII. The House, The Garden, And The Orchard

Our house, Ludwigshoehe #8, was not very large. It had two floors, a cellar and an attic. The first floor was covered with white stucco, the second floor was covered with wooden shingles, and the steep roof was covered with bright red tiles. Not much of it could be seen, because the house was covered with vines that turned into a blazing red in fall. In front of the living room was a veranda that was closed in by hedge roses which were a bright red, but so full of mildew that we did not use this veranda.

On the first floor were the living room, a dining room of moderate size, and a huge kitchen with a large range that also heated the water for the central heating. On the second floor were the children's bedroom, the parents' bedroom, the small room for Maria and Marie, and later, when we added the playroom for the children downstairs, a huge deck that we could not use year-round because it had a tin floor that was too hot in summer to walk on.

Aunt Ada's room, which later became my realm, and doubled as guest room, was in the attic. The house was furnished with very simple, rustic furniture. Next to the kitchen in the open air was a covered patio with a round table where we ate in summer. The garden had a picket fence.

The road was only a sandy trail, rutted by the cow-drawn wagons of the peasants, barely accessible by car. On the road in front of the house stood an old, branched-out walnut tree that belonged to the village. We used to lease the tree to pick the nuts, and I remember that we all had brown hands in fall, when we peeled the nuts for storage.

Papa put huge nails in the tree trunk so that we could climb up to the place where the tree branched out. There were so many places to sit that all of us could sit on the tree without being seen and without disturbing each other. It was my favorite place for reading.

Next to the house was a lawn with many rosebushes, bordered by strawberry edgings. In two corners of the garden were tree-shaded arbors with picnic tables and benches where we had coffee on Sundays, and were we children played during the week when we were not digging our big hole. The bulk of the garden was planted with vegetables, fruit trees and berries, except for the compost heap where we grew pumpkins.

Most of the work in the garden was done by two women from the village but when Papa came home early enough he used to water the vegetables as well as us children with the garden hose.

We had a septic tank that was emptied from time to time into a huge barrel that stood at a secluded spot, hidden by trees, ripening until it was ready to be used as fertilizer. We avoided this corner of the garden because of its evil smell, but Papa heroically filled the watering can from the mess to fertilize the vegetables while we children looked on, holding our noses. Floh and I observed our father's activities and one day Floh filled a watering can with mud and water and watered the flowers with it. Then he turned to me and asked, "Steffi, does it stink already?"

Mama, who never did any household chores, helped with cutting the bounty of the vegetable garden for canning. During the meager years it was always a problem to get enough sugar for the fruits, and much of the harvest had to be given away. But in later years, shelf upon shelf in the cellar was filled with jars of preserves as well as with apples and nuts.

We children liked to collect the freshly laid eggs every day, and enjoyed the little newly hatched chicks that Maria took away from the brooding hen until all the eggs were hatched. She kept them warm above the huge range and fed them with hard-boiled eggs. Sometimes, she let us hold the little yellow fluffy balls in our hands.

In the orchard was a small gazebo in which enormous yellow-jacket hornets had built their intricate nests. Once a year, Papa and his neighbors donned masks and protective suits and burned out the nests. We were stung several times and the stings were extremely painful. But, after many years, the hornets got tired of rebuilding their nests and left us in peace.

From then on, we furnished the gazebo with our dolls' furniture. I had inherited -- I don't remember from whom -- a doll's bed, a perambulator, wardrobe and dresser, and my dolls, together with Elvira's and Elfriede's dolls, were a large family. But we did not create an imaginary doll's world as our mothers had done. We were too much rooted in reality, and had too many other interests. I was mostly interested in sewing clothes and beddings from the samples of decorative material that I got from the furniture store.

When we moved back to Nuernberg in fall, 1922, we kept the orchard and converted the gazebo into a weekend cabin where we spent many happy days until we had to leave Germany.

VIII. Religion and Holidays

Our parents never emphasized religion. This does not mean that we were not taught basic moral values. We knew that we should not hurt anybody, we loved our parents dearly, we knew that we were loved and cherished, not only by our parents but by a large, extended family and we were taught to be honest and truthful. We did believe in a father in heaven, because our maids prayed simple prayers with us when they put us to bed. But our first formal introduction to religion, especially to Jewishness, came in school.

During my childhood, religion was part of the school curriculum. People paid church tax with their income tax, and designated the religious congregation to which their church tax should go. They were also free not to pay this tax. My parents, though not practicing their religion, paid the tax and indicated that they belonged to the liberal Jewish congregation.

Twice a week, our lesson plan read "religion." Then, the class would split up, and Jewish and Catholic children, the minorities, went to different classrooms, while a Protestant pastor came to the home room. The Catholic students were taught by a priest, and we had our own Jewish teacher. Our religion teacher was a cranky old woman, but I enjoyed her lessons. She belonged to the liberal Jewish congregation. A minority of Jewish students were members of the orthodox congregation which had a smaller synagogue, where they had their religious instruction after school.

Even observant Jews celebrated Christmas as a time for giving presents to their servants, and a holiday from work. But in our house, Christmas was celebrated with all the pomp of a Christmas tree. My parents, grandparents and the Ludwigs very seldom went to the synagogue or observed Jewish customs. They considered themselves Germans. My brothers also had no use for Jewish religion, though they received Jewish instruction in school and celebrated their Bar Mitz-vahs. Only I had an inborn need for formalized religion, and I learned the Jewish prayers in Hebrew with love and zest.

At home, we celebrated the Christian holidays without ever learning their religious significance. I insisted that we celebrate Chanukah instead of Christmas. I am still puzzled about my mother's reply, "We will celebrate Chanukah for your sake, but we will continue to celebrate Christmas, which is not only a Christian holiday, but the feast of the winter solstice, that our ancestors, the old Germans, celebrated when the days were getting longer again."

I was satisfied, but mystified, because our ancestors were the Jewish patriarchs Abraham, Isaac, and Jacob, as I had learned in school, and not the ancient German tribes.

We always had a Christmas tree, and the customary great table with gifts for everyone in the family, including servants, grandparents, and aunts Ada and Hede. Though we children received fewer gifts than our non-Jewish neighbors, and our tree was smaller than theirs -- they had huge Christmas trees from floor to ceiling -- it was a festive affair with rich gifts of clothing and bedding for the servants.

Maria was baking Christmas Stollen, fruitcakes made from rich yeast dough, and cookies all through December in preparation for the holidays, much to the delight of us, the watching, helping, and tasting children. Most of the goodies were given away to neighbors, the servants and their families, and many packages were sent to our Prussian relatives and to Papa's relatives in small communities in southern Germany.

Christmas Eve, we had to wait, like all German children, behind closed doors until the doors of the formal dining room were opened, and we could admire the candle-lit Christmas tree, sing a couple of carols, and finally find the place of our gifts and goodies on the huge table.

For many years we had our celebration in the late afternoon, and afterwards went to Papa's friend Zuern's house to celebrate with him, his wife and daughters. They had a tree from floor to ceiling, and a dinner of hot dogs and potato salad. After dinner we played with the two blonde, blue-eyed girls with their doll's house and doll's kitchen.

I, also, had a doll's house and a doll's kitchen, and the boys had a doll's grocery store, which was filled every Christmas with miniature fruits and vegetables made of marzipan, or, during the lean years, imitation marzipan. There were also tiny candies, packed in miniature replicas of commercial packages. Drawers were filled with raisins, nuts, and tiny pieces of chocolate. They sold their goods for real money to friends and family, saved their money, and finally bought an electric train with their profits. We were allowed to play with the doll's house, doll's kitchen, and the grocery store all through Christmas vacation. Then it was put away for the rest of the year.

We were singing the Christmas carols with all the references to Jesus, Mary and Joseph, but in our hearts we knew that these people did not belong to our religion. Our most memorable Christmas celebrations were those when we lived on the Ludwigshoehe, and we were snowed in, and all our guests had to stay overnight.

Most of the time, Easter coincided with the Jewish feast of Passover. We searched for our Easter eggs in the garden, and as long as we were small, did not even know about the Jewish holiday. Only after we had learned about Passover in school, were we sent to Uncle Issi or Uncle Salo for the seder.

For the seder, the family celebration of the exodus from Egypt, we each followed the ceremony in our little booklet, the Hagadah, most of the time unable to follow the celebrant, who read in Hebrew, while we read the German translation. The seder begins with questions about the significance of the strange customs of this night, questions which are asked by the youngest child who is able to memorize them in Hebrew. After the recitation, the child was rewarded with a present, most of the time a book.

Embedded in stories from the Talmud, the historic events were told and symbolized by the unleavened bread, the bitter herbs to remind us of the hardship the Israelites endured during their period as slaves in Egypt, and a brown, sweet concoction of apples, nuts and cinnamon that represented the mud, from which they had to form the bricks to build temples and palaces for the pharaoh.

When the celebrant blessed the first of the matzos, he broke it, wrapped half of it in a napkin, and put it aside for further use as dessert after the meal. This was the signal for the children to steal this piece of matzoh, the afikomen. After the long story was read, a sumptuous meal followed, accompanied by drinking of wine, even by the children. When the table had been cleared after the meal, the celebrant looked for his piece of matzoh, but it was gone. He had to ransom it from the child in possession of it after lengthy haggling for the price, because the seder could not continue without the afikomen.

The second part of the seder was very relaxed, because all the participants sang the traditional songs together, at a time when all already had too much wine.

I usually slept in Uncle Issi's or Uncle Salo's house after the seder, because it was too late to go to the Ludwigshoehe. After our cousin Kurt Ottensooser was married, the family seder took place in his house. He made the seder very interesting, asking questions and explaining the stories in German. The adults resented that his seder took so long, but I enjoyed answering his questions and learning more about the background of our celebration.

The Jewish feast of Shabuoth, which coincides with Pentecost, slipped away unnoticed. We usually made a trip during this short vacation from school.

New Year and Yom Kippur in the fall set us apart from our classmates, who had to go to school while we were given the days off. On these days, even non-practicing Jews went to the services. Our temple was not large enough to handle such a large congregation, and a hall was rented for an additional service. This hall was near grandmother's house, and though she never went to the temple during the year, she seldom missed the last part of the service on the Day of Atonement, the Yom Kippur. At the close of the service, the congregation three times repeats the statement, "Adonai, He Ho'elohim," the Lord is our God. The first time, it is sung timidly in a minor key, the second time with more strength, and the third time triumphantly in a major key. Then the shofar, the Ram's horn, sounds for the last time, and joy and peace of mind fills the hearts of the penitents who have fasted all day long.

This last statement summed up all of grandmother's religion. When we came home from the temple, even before eating she used to sit down at the piano and paraphrase the melody over and over again. The "Adonai He Ho'elohim" was the only piece of music I ever heard grandmother play, and at that occasion she taught me the difference between minor and major keys in music.

The Jewish religious year ends with Sukkoth, the feast of thanksgiving for the harvest, and at the same time, a remembrance of the long years that the children of Israel wandered around in the desert before entering the promised land. Orthodox Jews live during this week in flimsy huts built of twigs, like the ones the children of Israel used in the desert. Nobody in our family ever built a sukkah, a hut, but we did visit our friends and attended the blessing of wine and bread in the sukkah of our synagogue.

The last day of Sukkoth is the feast of Simchas Torah, the joy of the Torah, when the last chapter of the Torah is read, followed by the first chapter on the creation of the world. In Orthodox services, the men drink lots of wine and dance with the Torah in their arms. This was not done in our synagogue, so our cousin Betty usually took us with her to their small Orthodox synagogue in the Essenweinstrasse, where her family attended services.

In Betty's household, all the Jewish laws of eating Kosher were followed, which called for separation of meat and milk dishes, avoidance of pork, and strict observance of the special requirements during the Passover week, during which no ordinary bread or any fermented food, except wine, may be consumed. In our home we ate everything, and did not even observe the family celebration of the Friday evening, when bread, wine and all the children receive a special blessing. I insisted for a while that we have "kiddush," the blessing of wine and bread, and a festive meal on Friday night. This was a problem, because Papa never came home in time and we had to wait for him until Mama became so exasperated that we finally had to drop the festivities.

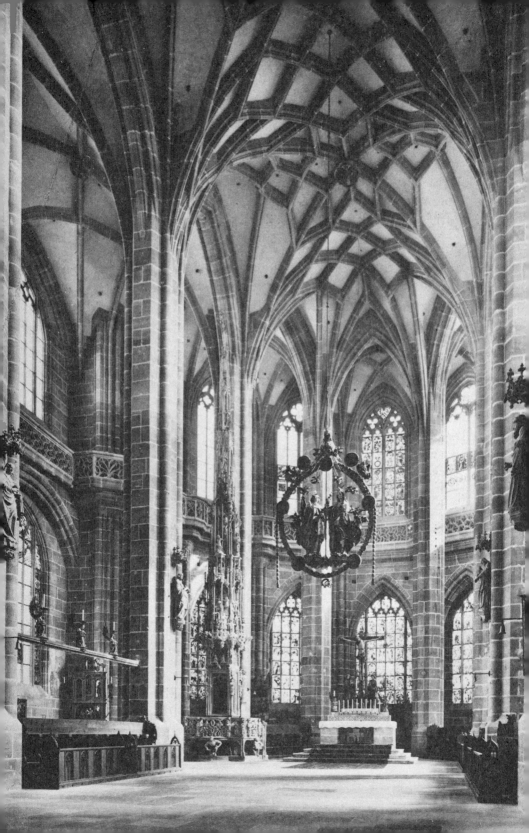

IX. Childhood Memories

I entered school in Fall 1918. It was a very short first grade because the system changed from school starting in September to school starting at Easter. We were all promoted to the next grade after eight months of school.

Mama did not want to enroll me in the village school in near-by Rueckersdorf. I went instead to the same private girls' school to which my mother and her sisters had gone. I was too small to go by train every day to the city, so it was decided that I had to stay in grandmother's house during the week, where poor Ada's bed was empty because she was in a psychiatric clinic after a suicide attempt. I went home only on weekends. My aunt Hede shared the room with me. This was no longer the opulent flat in which my mother grew up since Emilie and Arnold moved after the marriage of their daughters. It was a flat on the second floor of a big apartment house, with a salon, dining room, living room, a study, and two bedrooms.

The bathroom was dark and cold. I seldom took a bath there, because I took my weekly bath on weekends at home. At that time a bath every Saturday was considered plenty, when most houses didn't even have a bathroom. The kitchen was large and sunny, but the maid had only a dark cubicle of a room off the kitchen. Grandfather was sick and had retired. He had diabetes and spent most of the time lying on the sofa in the living room that used to be grandmother's domain. Grandmother was now sitting on a rocking chair at the bay window.

Food, my great preoccupation, was rationed, of bad quality, and in short supply. At home, we had the garden, the chickens, the rabbits, but grandmother's fare was sparse and drab. Only grandfather, with his special diet, had rare treats

The Church of St. Lorenz in Nuernberg.

and pure coffee. Aunt Hede was responsible for grandfather's food. She used to travel by train to neighboring farming communities, and like so many "Hamsterers," people who collected food like a hamster, she went from farm to farm to get eggs, sausages, butter, and sometimes a piece of meat for money and good words. I often went with her on weekends, though I hated begging for food and enduring the often sharp comments by the peasants and travellers on the train when we put our shopping bags on the luggage rack. Often enough, our loot was quite meager, and we had walked miles for nothing, or for just an egg or two. I had to cheer up my poor aunt, who was easily depressed.

Grandfather's sickness was very expensive, and his retirement income was not too good after he and his brother had sold their wholesale business in men's gloves and hats.

Aunt Hede, the daughter who had never had a chance to get a teacher's certificate, had a tutoring service in the study, off the living room. Students who had missed school because of sickness, or underachievers, came in the afternoon to do their homework under her supervision. In the mornings, she went to the houses of sick children to tutor them. I spent part of my afternoons in her classroom, disturbing her pupils or, later, when I could read, reading their textbooks. I had learned to read in a very short time, and became a bookworm ever after.

On our first day of school, we first had an air raid drill and then we went to our classroom. I had a very old teacher, who had been the first grade teacher of my mother and her sisters. Next to me sat Dorle Sontheimer, the daughter of one of my mother's good friends. I would not have chosen her for a friend, but our mothers told us to be best friends. Dorle, Heinz Bruckmann, Lily's son, and I had to play together at the behest of our mothers, either at the Sontheimer's or at the Bruckmann's apartment.

But we had a playground, too. The stables of the post office were between their house and grandmother's house. The mail in the city was still delivered by horse-drawn carriage, while the old stagecoaches were replaced by mail cars on the railway. Those old carriages stood broken down, rotting in the huge barn. We used to sit in one or the other of them and travel together to faraway places. Once, when my Ludwig cousins from Berlin were visiting, our games became more imaginative, because Elvira and Elfriede were more interesting than Dorle and Heinz, and because Elfriede was older than we were and knew more about the world. We had hair-raising adventures, crossing the vast mountains and prairies of America, fighting Indians, about whom we Nuernbergers knew nothing yet, but learned from our cousins from

The Mail Coaches on their way to deliver the mail in the early nineteen hundreds.

Berlin. When I see us sitting in the musty, dark coaches, I can smell the warm horses in their nearby stalls, the oats in the bins, and the oiled leather harnesses on the walls.

It was a German custom that a child got an oversized cardboard cone filled with candy as a present on his first day of school, as large or larger than the child himself. The new student was then sent to a photographer who took a picture of the child with his "Schultuete." We have no such pictures of ourselves, because it was wartime and all we received was a tiny bag of a few candies.

Nevertheless, first grade was fun with our dear old teacher who liked to play his violin and let us sing along. While reading and arithmetic were easy for me, penmanship was another story. I was unable to produce neat letters because, unknown to me or my parents, I had (and still have) a problem with coordination. I never knew why I could not catch a ball, skip rope, or play hopscotch like the other children. I was subjected to much mockery, punishment, and scolding for something I could not help, and I wept many bitter tears, yet could not improve my skills in spite of my superhuman efforts.

Soon after we started school, our school building was requisitioned by the military for a hospital, and all the girls of our school had to double up with the children of the nearby public elementary school. We had to go on double shift, one week in the morning, the next week in the afternoon. The children in the public school were less sheltered than we were, and their families suffered more from lack of soap and bathrooms than we did. Soon our heads were graced by little lice and nits. School was closed for a week while everybody tried to get rid of the little invaders.

For weeks, grandmother spread old newspapers in her lap and combed my hair with a fine-tooth comb to get rid of all the nits that had settled in my long, silky hair. Finally, she got fed up, took me to a beauty shop and had my curls cut, an act for which my mother never forgave her.

Grandfather grew weaker, and suffered from bedsores and had gangrene in his foot. While I was at grandmother's house, he had to have a leg amputated, and was in the hospital for a long time. I don't remember whether I ever talked with my grandfather, even in his better days. For me, he was a silent old man with whom I had no relationship. He died during the summer of 1919 while I was at home with my parents.

Aunt Ada was also at our home during the summer vacation. She had learned woodcarving as a part of her occupational therapy in the clinic. I liked to watch her as she carved picture frames with intricate arabesques of her own design.

When grandfather died, it was a relief for him and all the family, especially for poor Hede who had borne the brunt of his care. In September, when school reopened, grandfather was no longer lying on the sofa in the living room. Grandmother had not yet returned to her former resting place, but sat day in, day out on the rocking chair at the bay window where she could watch the people in the street. I often sat with her on the other, smaller rocking chair, while Hede was busy with her students.

Grandfather's bed was now empty, and grandmother invited me early in the morning to come to her in the big bed. She enticed me by reciting, with great skill, ballads that she knew by heart. The hours in her bed were a delight and an ordeal. Grandmother had a weak heart and took tincture of valerian in great amounts. Later, I realized that it was the alcohol in the mixture that made it so attractive to her. For me, the strong smell of valerian was quite repulsive.

Another ordeal during the winter of 1919 was the cod liver oil that we poor children had to gulp every day. The food was terrible. Even potatoes were in short supply and we ate turnips, which I hated, instead of potatoes.

But there were also silver linings. Grandmother regretted all her life, or, rather, during all the vacations to the Baltic Sea, that she could not swim. We had a heated indoor municipal swimming pool not far from grandmother's house. We went there together twice a week. Grandmother watched with great satisfaction as I learned how to swim. During spring and early summer, grandmother liked to go to a garden cafe with me, where she met with her friends while all the children played together in the playground.

When I lived again at home during the summer of 1920, Mama spent more time with us children than ever before. She could not go as often as she liked to Nuernberg because she was still in mourning for her father and Ada could not come home to spend the summer with us because she was too sick. Mama often went to visit her in the clinic for a few days, and was very depressed when she returned home.

Mama was also depressed for another reason. She saw very little of Papa. Papa left at seven in the morning and returned after seven at night, or later. He also tried to sell furniture in Holland and made frequent trips to Holland.

For us, that is, for Floh and me, the fatherless evenings were a source of delight, because Mama read all the books to us that she herself had enjoyed as a child. She could read very vividly. I can remember all of them, starting with Jules Verne's "Around the World in Eighty Days," continuing with "Little Lord Fauntleroy," "Tom Sawyer," " Huckleberry Finn," and the sad tale of Remi in "Sans Famille" by Hector Maillot.

We had just started this book when Papa decided it was time for a vacation with his two older children. The little boys were left with our help Maria and Marie, and we took off for a five-day hiking trip through the Frankonian Swiss, a lovely, small mountain chain north of Nuernberg.

Papa, Floh and Steffi on the trip through the Frankonian Swiss.

It was the first time that both parents spent time with Floh and me, and it was uninterrupted bliss to learn to know that delightful stranger who was our father. We saw stalactite caves, ruins of medieval castles, a lovely baroque church, a geological museum with fossils from long-ago days. We hiked in the valleys and climbed hills. We ate the fresh trout from the mountain brooks and slept in heavy feather beds in rural inns. All the while, Mama continued to read "Sans Famille" to us. Even Papa listened when, through her well-modulated voice, every character came to life, each with his distinctive way of speaking.

One unforgettable afternoon we sat under a bridge, next to a tumbling, murmuring mountain brook, nestled against Mama's soft and warm body, as she read the chapter in Sans Famille about the disaster in the coal mine, when Remi and his companions were buried for two weeks until the rescuers arrived. And all the while, while Remi was starving, we were munching chocolates.

I soaked in the new experience like a dry sponge, and every minute of this trip was euphoric bliss, while our parents discovered with a vengeance how much fun children could be. Papa, who liked to lecture, found a captive audience for his teaching, and from then on he took us more often on all kinds of excursions.

During the summer of 1920, while Hans Ludwig was serving as medical orderly on the Russian front, Toni struggled along in Berlin with her three daughters. They had little money, and less food, and could not often come to Nuernberg. But when Hans returned from the war, he did not want to return to his old job as reporter for the Berlin Morning Post, but wanted to have a business of his own. It happened that my father's most encompassing hobby was to establish new businesses; he had done so for his brother Simon, for his brother-in-law Salo Gans, and for his nephew Albert Rosenfelder. Now he found another prey for his quest. All the enterprises he created were in the field of furniture manufacturing and selling. For Hans, who had very little capital to invest, he suggested furniture accessories. To the great joy of Martha and Toni, he invited Hans to live near us, so that he could help him with introductions, as well as knowledge in his new field. The Ludwigs moved to the Ludwigshoehe, where Hans started a mail-order business.

He sold door locks, knobs for drawers and doors, glue-on ornaments made of horn, metal, wood turned on the lathe or, later, made of plastic. His warehouse of thousands of little articles in boxes and pigeonholes filled one room of the small apartment that they had rented, on top of the hill above our house.

Their house was a Victorian villa with turrets and a steep roof with multicolored roof tiles. The house had become too big for the owners after their children grew up and had moved away. The Ludwigs lived on the second floor, with their maid who did the housework, while Toni helped her husband in his new business. Their quarters were very cramped, but it did not disturb them much during the summer because we children played day in, day out in the wonderful forest that stretched between our houses and far beyond. We loved this mixed forest with its evergreens and its deciduous trees that changed colors in fall, with its wildflowers, berries, and wildlife. The three Ludwig girls who had lived in the city all their lives enjoyed the yard with the chickens, the pigs, and a huge vegetable and fruit garden. Though they were not allowed to pick berries and fruits, they did so anyway, feeling pleasurably guilty about their transgressions.

The Ludwigs did not have a telephone, and the distance between our houses was too great for shouting to each other. So Toni and Martha had found a means of communication by yodeling, which they had developed into an intricate code.

We five children went for long walks, always with Fritz as our protector, though the poor dog had to leave us sometimes to go about his own business of chasing rabbits and deer. Then we would go home without him, and he came home later cowering, guiltily expecting punishment.

One bright Sunday morning we set out together with Fritz. We picked berries and followed the patch further and further, until we were in unknown territory and did not know the way home. Fritz was gone. By then, the sky was covered with clouds, and it was dark in the deep forest. We knew that the side of the tree that was covered with moss was west, but we did not know which direction our house was in. The two little ones, Irene and Floh, began to cry, and even we three older girls were panic stricken. At last we saw Fritz, far away between the trees. We called him but he ran from us. We followed him, but whenever we came nearer, he went on before we caught up with him. This went on until we reached the little brook with the tiny lake that we used often as a swimming hole. Now, Fritz stood still, and we petted and thanked him for leading us. We went on through the gorge with the overhanging cliffs that were so familiar to us from our games, and soon reached home.

The wonderful summer drew to its end. I continued to live in Nuernberg with grandmother, but Elfriede and Elvira were sent to the village school in Rueckersdorf.

Because they were much better educated than the peasant children, they both were able to skip a grade, and were quite happy in the new surroundings, except on cold days when they had to climb the steep hill in the snow on their way home from school.

Ada was in a deep depression all through the winter of 1919 and through 1920. I think the last time I saw her was in 1919. She was in a clinic near Frankfurt, where she was given occupational therapy and treated with drugs. Mama said that Ada was even thinner than she was before, but she still had happy interludes when Stephan came to visit her. They made plans for the future, when Stephan was a doctor, and would make her strong and healthy again.

It was not to be. Wild attacks of despair and agitation alternated with times of deep melancholy. In November 1920, Mama received a phone call informing her that the people at the clinic could not handle Ada any longer, and that she should be taken to an asylum.

Papa was on one of the his frequent trips to Holland. Toni wanted to go with Hans, but Mama wanted to be with her favorite sister in the hour of need and one of the sisters had to stay with the children. Mama and Hans went together. Ada was calm when they arrived. They packed her belongings and returned on the train back to Nuernberg. Ada became violent on the train, and in Nuernberg they asked for the assistance of a police escort which took them directly to a police station. While Mama and Hans were filling out forms, Ada grabbed a saber that was hanging on the wall and stabbed herself hari-kari style in the abdomen. She died in the ambulance on the way to the hospital. Mama said later, "You should have seen the look of triumph in her face when she had fooled all of us, and finally succeeded in one of her many suicide attempts.''

All the family was badly shaken by the events. Each of them felt guilty for having failed her. Toni and Mama blamed their mother for most of Ada's misery, but grandmother steadfastly maintained that it was not her fault. Possibly in her deepest conscience, she felt remorseful and perhaps as a result of this, though only 62 years old, acted like a very old woman. She walked heavily with a cane, stopping frequently, and once, to my embarrassment, had a fainting spell while she was walking with me. She fell in the street. Bystanders came and helped her back to her feet and she was able to walk home. Actually, I was more shaken than she.

1920-1921 was the last winter in grandmother's house. She enjoyed long conversations with me in which I learned about her political views. She was very upset by the revolution when the German emperor and all the little kings and dukes of Germany had to abdicate, including the Austrian emperor Franz Joseph and King Ludwig III of Bavaria. She also told me of the history of our beautiful Nuernberg, which had once been the site of the German Reichstag and had been the home of the most famous artists, such as Albrecht Durer, Viet Stoss, and Adam Kraft, and was the home of the only German poet-- Hans Sachs--during the time of the Meistersinger, when craftsmen like Hans Sachs, a shoemaker, dominated the literary scene in Germany.

Nuernberg, glorious years as a free city state, came to an end about 1800 when it became a part of Bavaria. But the pride of its citizens had conserved the beautiful gothic churches, the palaces of its wealthy merchants, the castle on top of the hill and the ancient city walls. Nuernberg jumped into the industrial age with large factories and an ever increasing population of factory workers, but all the new factories and tenements were built in the southern part of the town, leaving the old city in its long established beauty. Finally the old city of Nuernberg was completely bombed out in World War II. Yet, it was rebuilt according to the old plans and today, it is again one of the most harmonic testimonies to medieval architectural glory.

Grandmother used to tell me about the rich merchants, the patricians who had a monopoly in the trade of pepper for northern Germany, and sent their wagon trains to Venice, back to Nuernberg, and from there distributed it to the rest of the German countries. During this time, the pepper merchants, called peppersacks, were immensely rich, and adorned their city with beautiful churches, buildings, the first old-people's home, and wonderful fountains. Nuernberg was

The "Holy Ghost," old-people's home.

once called the jewelry box of the Holy Roman Empire of the German Nation, and its works of art, toys, and honey and pepper cakes were sent all over Europe.

Several times grandmother went with me to the German National Museum where I was most fascinated by the collection of doll houses which were not only playthings for the rich girls, but a means to learn their household chores. But grandmother was not my only companion when I was in Nuernberg, away from my parents. All my uncles and aunts took turns inviting me. I was not overly fond of going to their houses, but I had to. I liked my aunt Ida Ottensooser, and my uncle Eugen who had cancer of the throat and could only talk in a whisper. But, of their sons, Fritz the older was very aloof and rarely talked to a little girl like me, and the younger of them, Ernst, was emotionally disturbed, autistic, though highly intelligent, and I was afraid of him. Nevertheless, he was a master of chess and taught me to play the game.

The other Ottensooser families invited me frequently to their homes. Aunt Martha was sweet, but her children teased me cruelly. They always shouted ''Steffi with the green hair'' as soon as they saw me. I was conscious of my extraordinary hair color because grandmother had told me that, in the Middle Ages, redheads were considered to be witches and were burned at the stake, and I had enough humiliation when the kids in the street called after me, ''Red fox, your hair is afire, put a pail of water on it.''

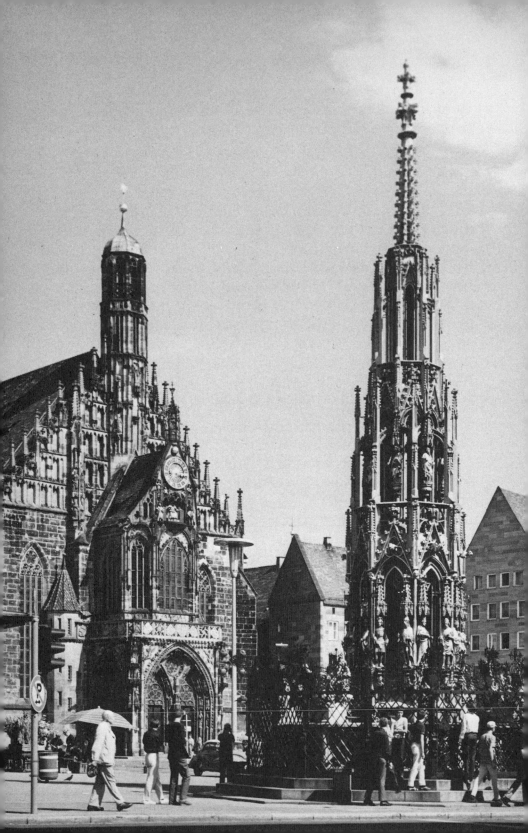

X. Kaleidoscope 1919-1922

As I try to recall my childhood, pictures appear in my mind, keeping me awake at night, haunting me, shifting, recurring in slightly different form, regardless of chronology or importance, worrying me because of missing parts, satisfying me because they are so happy. They prevent me from sleeping until I get up and write down at least a heading. I don't know how important it is to write about the incidents and impressions, but at least these fleeting memories will stop disturbing my nights after I write about them.

THE COACH

The furniture from our store was delivered in a horse-drawn wagon with the "The Braun Brothers" in big letters on its side. The horses, two brown mares, Lotte and Liesel, were stabled in a courtyard of a building that housed a small factory of my father's creation that had produced little pillows for soldier's helmets during the war, and that was now rented to working-class people as cold-water flats. The coachman, Herr Schuemel, lived in one of the flats. One nice day my father announced that he had received in trade a comfortable horse-drawn coach in payment for furniture. The coach was used on Sundays by one or the other Braun family, and we always felt like members of the nobility when we rode in it. Herr Schuemel would groom Lotte and Liesel until they shone, and would dress up in his Sunday best with a high stovepipe hat on his head. Whenever it was our turn to use the coach, my parents invited their friends and one child at a time was allowed to come along, sitting up front with the coachman.

Herr Schuemel was a great sport, letting us wield the long whip, shout "hue" and "hot," left and right for German horses, and sometimes even let us hold the reins. Elvira was Herr Schuemel's favorite. She would visit him in the stable whenever she was in Nuernberg and give sugar to the horses.

The Market Place with the Church of Our Lady and the "Golden Fountain."

The coach.

When Lotte and Liesel grew old, they were replaced by two roan geldings, named Max and Moritz after the characters from the German humorist Wilhelm Busch, but I did not love them as much as the two mares, and neither did Mr. Schummel. One memorable excursion included grandmother, Aunt Hede, Mama and three children; Floh, Irene and me. We drove to grandmother's birthplace, Baiersdorf, where she showed us the house in which she lived during the first happy years of her life, and where her father David had his porcelain factory. Afterwards we went to the cemetery where our ancestors were buried, and where Mama took pictures of the tombs.

The coach was sold when the family bought their first automobile, a Swiss-made Thurikum, an open car similar to Ford Model A, but the furniture was still delivered by the horse-drawn wagon.

WOODEN SHOES

During the war we did not manufacture furniture, and even the retail store business was very slow. Papa bought a ramshackle building between Nuernberg and its sister town Fuerth, where he made wooden clogs and sandals that were worn by soldiers, and later, when leather was in short supply, by everybody else. We children clip-clopped all during the war years in our wooden sandals, which were comfortable and cheap.

During the years of the German revolution in 1919, the workers wanted to unionize, but Papa was not yet ready to have a union shop. Some disgruntled workers set fire to our factory. It was a spectacular fire; only a few nails were left of the building, and some melted-down metal. Actually, it was not a disaster. Nobody got hurt, and with the money from the insurance the factory was moved to a large building near the municipal garden in Fuerth where expensive furniture was produced that was sold in the store or exported to Holland.

THUNDERSTORMS

I was lying in my little room in the garret of our house, the same room that was once Aunt Ada's domain which I had inherited after her death. It was a tiny room with two cots, a small closet, a desk, one chair, and slanting walls.

Suddenly, a loud noise startled me from my sleep. Sitting up, I hit my head on the slanting wall and slipped out of bed to sit on the desk and look out of the window. Fireworks of lightning crisscrossed the sky behind the silhouettes of the trees. Thunder shook the house to its foundations. I counted the seconds between lightning and thunder, and knew that the storm was very near. Fascinated by the beautiful spectacle, I could have sat there indefinitely, but Mama came up the stairs, grabbed me from my perch and dragged me downstairs to her bed where the window shades hid the lightning, and the thunder sounded much more frightening. She said, "I cannot understand why you are not afraid" while she lay shivering next to me.

I loved thunderstorms, which raged every year throughout the month of May, sometimes hitting the telephone poles, sometimes the lightning rod that protected our isolated house. Whenever the lightning came down on the wire of the lightning rod, we saw its flash through the window, and the house shook like in an earthquake and sent yowling Fritz under the sofa.

At that time I embarked on my writing career with a poem about a thunderstorm.

FOOD

Our cook Maria was an expert chef and served delicious dinners to our guests. On weekends, she would bake mountains of cakes, as if she had to supply a pastry shop. But Maria did not like to cook humdrum everyday fare, when nobody was there to praise her exquisite work. Our weekday dinners were lusterless and indifferent. She also prepared our brown-bagged school lunches without love or imagination. It was either liverwurst or soft metwurst with margarine and nothing else, not a candy, not a pickle, not an apple.

Mama was a gourmet and a gourmand. She loved to eat. She especially loved sweets and fancy chocolates. She was grossly overweight, and, on top of this, she never wore a bra or a girdle in that corsetted day and age. She knew that she looked a mess, but kept on munching candy while reading or sewing. We children looked on with watering mouths and envious eyes. Sometimes she would give us a tiny morsel, but more likely she would scold us for counting her bites.

We were trained to see our elders eat better food than our fare. At noon everybody ate the same dinner, but at the evening meal, when we ate our sandwiches of liverwurst or sandwich spread with margarine, or a thin slice of cheese, drinking watery tea with milk, Mama and Papa gorged themselves on platters of cold cuts, ham, a variety of cheese, and beer.

Of course, we were not starved, because the garden yielded berries, apples, plums, cherries, and pears, and we ate wild strawberries, blueberries, and blackberries in the forest after we had dutifully picked mushrooms for the dinner table.

After our Sunday guests had their fill of coffee and cake in our garden, they usually had a cold supper in the garden restaurant at the foot of the hill near the train station before taking the train back home. They often invited us children to join them and share with them the delicious sausages that Herr Schmidt, the innkeeper, made for the restaurant. Herr Schmidt was the fattest man I have ever seen. His belly dropped nearly to his knees.

From time to time, Mama went on a diet. On such occasions, she stayed in bed nearly all day long, which was fine, because her mood during dieting was harder on us than seeing her munching her candies. Fortunately, her periods of dieting were short, and after a few weeks of misery Mama ate again to her heart's content and loved us again.

THE PEGNITZ

Nuernberg's river is the Pegnitz. It begins in Upper Franconia, wending its way between forested mountains and through small medieval towns and picturesque villages, quite unpolluted until it reaches the industrial outskirts of Nuernberg.

It is a small, now unimportant river that was a busy highway in the Middle Ages because it was navigable for river barges as far as the Netherlands. Nuernberg is also connected by a canal to the river system of the Danube. This waterway from the Black Sea to the Netherlands contributed to Nuernberg's importance in history.

Nobody can swim in the Pegnitz in Nuernberg, where it is polluted, but near our home on the Ludwigshoehe it was clear. Twenty minutes from our home was a little bathhouse that we used whenever we went swimming. The river ran swiftly around a bend and when we crossed the stream near the bathhouse, we had a long, pleasant downstream swim around the bend.

Soon after I had learned to swim, from the lessons in the municipal pool, I swam around the bend but got caught in an eddy and nearly drowned. I lost consciousness and woke up on the grass with many people around me, after a stranger had pulled me out of the water.

We continued to swim in this place later when we did not live any longer on the Ludwigshoehe, but at that later time nobody swam there any longer because the river was so dangerous.

Near the Ludwigshoehe the valley of the Pegnitz is wide, surrounded by fields, meadows and swamps, but later the mountains ascend right next to the river, and each of the many stations on our train line is the starting point of lovely hiking trails. Throughout our childhood, first with parents and later with our youth groups, we hiked through the mountains, visited the old ruins of medieval castles, went to caves with stalagmites, waded in little brooks, picked rosehips, berries and mushrooms, taking the train that passed through Ludwigshoehe. Very often, we took Fritz along. He got a different ticket, a Hundekarte, a dog's ticket, on the train, and liked the train ride very much, except for one stretch with a number of tunnels, which apparently reminded him of his service in the war.

KERMESS
Every village had a big fair and carnival on the anniversary of the consecration of its church. Larger towns with more than one church had several fairs, one for each church.

During the week of the fair, the main street of each village was lined with rides and booths. The same carousel with its wooden horses went from one place to the other. It had a calliope and was pushed by roustabouts who drank many steins of beer between the rides.

A special pastry of yeast dough fried in oil, little kermess cakes, were eaten in the cafes and restaurants with coffee by the women, while the men drank beer.

LAUF ON THE PEGNITZ

About two miles from our house was an old town with medieval city gates, an old castle, and two railway stations. It was the market town for a large district, and was quite busy. The Pegnitz divided the town in two sections: Lauf, right of the Pegnitz, was where our train stopped after the Ludwigshoehe, and Lauf, left of the Pegnitz which was on a different train line.

Emilie's birthplace. Steffi, Aunt Hedwig, Grandmother, Irene and Floh.

Ottensoos, the town from which the family of my great grandfather David Ottensooser originated, was left of the Pegnitz. One nice summer day, Mama decided to go with Ada and me to Ottensoos. She was very interested in our family history. I don't remember anything about the trip, but I do remember that on our way back to the railway station we were caught in a thunderstorm and downpour that drenched us to the skin. We lost our way and nearly drowned in the swamp around the village.

I had forgotten the incident until I read David Ottensooser's diary. There he describes a visit to Ottensoos when he lost his way and nearly drowned in the big swamp around the village.

Every outing to Lauf with Mama was crowned by a visit to a cafe or restaurant where we got coffee and cakes, and, after the war years, whipped cream or ice cream. I especially remember a cafe with exquisite pastry, usually our last stop before going home. We sometimes took the train for the short hop to Lauf, but more often we walked either in the valley or across the mountain, heavily laden on the way home by our purchases. We went to Lauf quite often because our seamstress and our family doctor lived there.

ERNA BRAUNGER

Papa often travelled to Holland while establishing his furniture export business. After a few years of making business connections in Holland, he invited his Dutch friends to visit him in Germany, and while they were in Nuernberg he invited them for a big dinner to the Ludwigshoehe. Mama, who was reluctant to be the only woman at the table with five men, invited a neighbor, Erna Braunger, a piano teacher, one of the unmarried women of the lost generation. Mama did not know her well but had observed her at the train station as a beautiful, animated woman.

The four guests arrived by train, four serious young men in dark business suits. My parents and Erna met them at the station, and we soon sat down for a sumptuous dinner. Maria had outdone herself. It was a gourmet affair featuring roast duck with all the trimmings, and plenty of wine. We children got our small share of wine, diluted with water. But the dessert, called "drowned virgins" was a concoction of pastry in a wine sauce. It was quite strong, and we children each ate a large portion of it as did the adults.

Everybody, including the children and the previously so serious Dutch friends, became pleasantly drunk.

We never had seen our parents so merry. The house shook with our laughter. Instead of the distant, formal "Sie" all of them suddenly used the informal, intimate address of "Du." When the party was over, our guests were again strangers except for Mama and Erna, who became intimate friends, to the jealous displeasure of Lily, who resented her rival.

Mama's friendship with Erna continued when we moved to Nuernberg since by that time Erna had also moved there. She became Floh's piano teacher, and was a frequent visitor who had lunch with us once a week. She was a wonderful person whom we loved and admired.

She, like so many of her age group, could not stand the lonely, virginal life, and had a long-lasting affair with a married man. At the dinner table, with us children present, she would pour out her problems and frustrations to Mama --an early sex education for me, who listened avidly.

Erna, who was not Jewish, was never taken in by Hitler, and she and Mama stayed close friends even after the Nazis took over Germany, and after we had left Germany her letters were treasured by all of us.

But her story was quite sad because she, a piano teacher, developed arthritis in her hands later in her life and could play no more. Her married friend reconciled with his wife and left her. After the war, we heard that she had died a lonely and bitter death.

MY LITTLE BROTHERS

Floh and I, so close together in age, not only became close playmates, but we later shared our daily train ride to school and our many excursions into the forest with Fritz. Our two little brothers Heinz and Werner played no role in our lives; it was as if they belonged to a separate generation.

Heinz pulled his little wooden wagon through the garden, all by himself, until Werner was old enough to become a passenger. Werner had finally outgrown his baby carriage in which he stood neglected on the balcony for the first year of his life. The two little boys played together, ignored by the grownups. Heinz grew sturdy and strong. Grandmother used to call him her "little woodsman," but Werner, maybe as a result of his early benign neglect, developed asthma.

In 1921, when Werner was three years old, the doctor recommended a lengthy stay by the sea. My mother, who had such fond memories of her childhood vacations on the Baltic Sea, was delighted by prescription. Papa said there was not enough money for the whole family to go, so she took Werner and Floh, who was frail and tiny for his age, and departed for Brunshaupten at the Baltic Sea.

Mama had a wonderful vacation, while Floh and Werner got to know one another and played together on the beach. To crown the trip, Papa joined them for a few days in Brunshaupten, before they returned home tanned and in high spirits.

I had not missed them very much because I had stayed with grandmother and Hede during their absence, and was fully occupied with friends and school. It was another story for four-year-old Heinz who was left alone with the servants, abandoned by parents and brothers. He felt rejected and lonely without understanding the reason.

In spring of 1922, the doctor again suggested a vacation for the little asthma sufferer. This time he recommended a mountain climate. Mama traveled again with Floh and Werner. Their destiny was Meran in the Dolomites, part of the Alps that once belonged to Austria, but was given to Italy after World War I. The three of them had a lovely vacation. I did not mind their absence very much but Heinz was completely shattered by the experience of being left behind a second time.

Mama must have realized that her early neglect of Heinz was cruel of her, because in her later years, Heinz was her great favorite and a deep friendship developed between them, especially after Papa's death. As a matter of fact, we often jokingly called Heinz our "Oedipus" because of his great attachment to his mother.

The trip became a wonderful memory for them but Werner's asthma did not get better, and Floh did not grow or gain weight.

XI. Maria and Marie

When we winterized our summerhouse in 1919 and lived the whole year round on the Ludwigshoehe, our cook refused to move out of the city and face the loneliness of country life, and we had to hire a new cook.

Maria Winkler, who came to us with the best references, was born in Rosenberg, a small town in the Oberpfalz with large iron mines and blast furnaces where the people of the village found employment. Maria was cook in an officer's mess in Amberg, a city near Rosenberg with a large military base, where she had learned to cook gourmet meals for large groups of people.

Sunday morning on the Ludwigshoehe.

It was still starvation time in Germany. There was little sugar, no cream, no butter. However, we had chickens, and she could whip up the most delicious desserts and icings with egg whites and the fruits of our garden.

Maria was in her late twenties when she joined us. She had a big goiter, a sallow complexion, and straight, black, oily hair.

Nevertheless, she had a boyfriend, Fritz Pfau. Fritz had a wife in Belgium whom he married when he was a soldier in the army and from whom he could not get divorced because he was Catholic. He and Maria had to "live in sin." Maria was also Catholic and was deeply disturbed about the fact that she was a sinner who could not take holy communion, and would go straight to hell if she died. But love was stronger than the threat of damnation.

Fritz was short, stout, and bowlegged, with a large mustache, a huge nose, and black hair. He often spent weekends in our house, and neither we children nor our parents worried about their sleeping arrangement. Once our parents went for a long trip and were happy that Fritz stayed in our house as our protector. We children used to call him our vice-father, and he gave the little boys the love and attention that they craved. Fritz or Maria did not go for walks with us, nor did they take us to the city or read to us or tell us stories as our mother did, but Fritz was full of fun, games and jokes and we loved him dearly.

Soon after Maria came to us, our maid got sick and tired of country life. Probably Maria, with her dour disposition, was giving her a hard time. She was replaced by Marie, a friend of Maria's from the same village.

Marie Reber was the one who raised my little brothers. The two babies left her little time for household chores, and Mama had to hire additional help for housecleaning, laundry and garden work.

Two peasant women from the nearby village, Ruckersdorf, Frau Buettner and Frau Seitz were the best of friends, and always came to us together. They were typical peasant women, dressed in the old-fashioned way with long black skirts and bandannas.

Frau Buettner was married. Her husband tended to their meager farm. They had one cow, which drew the farm

Fran Buettner and Frau Seitz.

wagon and also supplied milk for the family. The fields were outside the village, but the house, stable and barnyard were in the village in an old house with timbered framework. Frau Buettner never opened the windows, and the air in the house, like in other peasant homes, was stale and oppressive.

Frau Seitz was a widow with an only son, Gustel. Gustel was a very bright youngster, and when he finished school my father took him into the business as an apprentice. He stayed with my father through thick and thin, and even stayed on with the Nazi who later bought our factory for a song. Gustel did this in order to look after Papa's rights. When the war ended, Gustel testified in court that Papa was the real owner of the factory and the business was returned to him, with Gustel's help.

Marie, the maid, was younger and prettier than Maria. She was petite with golden blonde hair and blue eyes. It was inevitable that she eventually left us to get married.

Her wedding in Rosenberg was a big event for all of us. Mama and the four children stayed for two days in the large old farmhouse owned by Maria's brother. The Catholic ceremony with a mass in the simple village church was a new experience that impressed me very much. The wedding feast afterwards was merry. We had music and dancing, and we children were allowed to eat to our hearts' content, and to drink wine.

The highlight of our visit, however, was not the wedding but a visit to the blast furnace during the evening. Maria's boyfriend Fritz who worked there, took us and explained every step of the process. We arrived at the blast furnace at exactly the critical moment when it was opened and the fiery, molten iron ran out into the earthenware forms on the floor where it gradually thickened into hard bars. Our arrival at the furnace had been carefully timed by Fritz.

Henceforth, whenever we learned in school about steelmaking, I proudly related my unforgettable experience. Much later, when I was a teacher, I even told my students about it.

Maria and Fritz Pfau.

Many years later, Marie died in giving birth to her fourth child. Her husband married for a second time, and we never heard from him again.

While we lost track of Marie's offspring, Maria stayed with us for many years.

Once she got pregnant and had an abortion. Mama went with her to the clinic and cared for her because, by now, she and Mama were intimate friends and she was considered part of our family.

Her pregnancy was the last straw in her relationship with Fritz. She finally broke up with him and went to confession. Afterwards, she told Mama, "Now, when I die, I will only go to purgatory, but I am worried about you. You are not a Christian, and do not believe in Jesus. You will go directly to hell."

XII. A Trip with Mama and Lily

It was a time-honored custom that women had to wear black for a full year after the death of a close relative. They gradually eased into their normal way of dressing by adding white to their mourning outfits for a period of transition. Men wore a black armband around a sleeve. But both men and women were expected to refrain from entertainment such as dancing, parties, theaters, concerts, or movies during the time of mourning.

After grandfather's death, the family observed the full ritual of mourning. Mama had just added white trim to her black dresses when the tragedy of Ada's suicide put them all back in severe black.

Mama was shattered by the loss of her favorite sister, but observing a whole year of mourning for Ada was too much for her. She resumed her outings with her friend Lily Bruckmann. Once a week she took the late morning train to Nuernberg. There, she and Lily had a gourmet lunch together, and in the afternoon they went clandestinely to a movie. Mama was afraid that acquaintances would see them in a movie theater and start their tongues wagging about her irreverence. So, they never went to a movie theater in the center of town, but patronized obscure little moviehouses in the suburbs, which were less fashionable, but where they were secure from being recognized.

Lily had become more masculine looking with the years. She was one of the first society ladies to bob her hair. She used to dress in severe marine-blue suits with shirt-like white blouses, and a dark fuzz grew under her huge aquiline nose. She could not conceal her sex completely because a heavy girdle pushed her ample bosom upwards and made it very conspicuous.

Besides Mama's weekly trips to Nuernberg, Lily used to visit Mama at least once a week in our country house, all too often accompanied by her son Heinz, whom we considered a spoiled brat. Wolfgang and I did not like Heinz, but we were forced by our mothers to play--or fight--with him.

During the trip with our parents to the Franconian Swiss a few years earlier, we visited a beautiful cave which was called the Bing Hoehle, because it was discovered by a member of the wealthy Bing family of Nuernberg. Our mother explained to us that the Bing family owned many factories. In our imagination we created a Frau Bing who was a powerful woman, and we were her slaves. She gave us tasks that we had to fulfill.

The most ambitious of our labors was to dig a hole so deep that it would end in Australia on the other side of the earth. Every day, as soon as we were alone together, one of us would go down into the hole and dig, while the other would remove the earth and hide it somewhere in the garden. After we finished a day's work, we would cover the hole with a plank that we covered with earth, so that nobody would know about our work. We did not share the secret of our imaginary boss with anybody.

Heinz was definitely not the person to share our secret. His visits were unwelcome interruptions in our hole-digging labors.

One day, after Lily and Heinz had recuperated from nasty colds, they decided that they had to get away from it all, and invited Mama, Floh and me to accompany them for a vacation at a very posh resort in the hills. The two little boys stayed at home under the care of Maria and Marie.

The hotel was very elegant, and the ladies feared that the three noisy children would disturb the other guests. We were asked to play far away in the neglected park of the hotel while Mama and Lily were lying on deck chairs on the sunny veranda, gossiping to their heart's content. We went downhill until we found a deserted gazebo, surrounded by high trees and dense bushes. It was after a warm summer rain, and the damp place smelled of decaying leaves.

The three of us played peacefully together as we had never done before, and after we finished with the routine games of pirates and princes, cops and robbers, and cowboys and Indians, Heinz suggested that we play doctor. We knew that this was a forbidden game, but we went along with his plan. We found nothing wrong with our operations, bandaging, transporting and feeding the patient in our dank gazebo hospital, and wondered why it was a forbidden game.

When we were finally called to dinner we sat subdued at the big table with all the guests and behaved perfectly, to the joy of our mothers. We were tired from the afternoon's exertions and went early to bed.

Mama and Lily shared one room, and we had an adjoining room with three beds. Mama and Lily seemed to have been talking most of the night and overslept. When they finally woke up, they were amazed that we had not disturbed them, and went to our room. There, they found the three of us sitting innocently and peacefully in my bed, playing cards.

Now the two ladies became suspicious because we were all found in the same bed. They feared the worst, and started a memorable fight about whose children had seduced whose children. The three of us were dumbfounded, because we were not aware of having done anything wrong this morning.

Mama had Floh and me dress immediately and, without breakfast, took the next train home, overwhelmed by shame. It took a few weeks until the incident was forgotten, and Mama and Lily resumed their friendship as if nothing had happened. Floh and I were again Frau Bing's faithful slaves, and Heinz was again our enemy.

XIII. School

My Aunt Ada committed suicide when I was in third grade. My teacher was the loveliest young girl I ever had. She was tall, slim, and had honey-colored hair, just as Aunt Ada did, except that she was healthy and happy. I transferred all my love for my lost aunt to Miss Lange.

Once, while walking in the park with grandmother, we met her, and I threw myself passionately into the arms of my teacher. Grandmother was mortified because it was so much out of step with the prevailing concept of respect and formal distance in the attitude towards teachers. Grandmother stood speechless as I hugged and kissed Fraulein Lange, and later she scolded me for my behavior.

Fraulein Lange used to invite one group of students after another to her house on Saturday afternoons for games and treats. She also took us for walks through the city, and once we took a field trip to our home in the Ludwigshoehe. Mama treated the whole class royally to cake and lemonade, a tour of the garden, the poultry yard and the rabbit cages. My classmates had always admired my beautiful rabbit fur, hat and muff, and were happy to cuddle and pet the lovely creatures that would later enrich our poor wartime diet.

When I started 4th grade, Floh and I took the train to Nuernberg daily together.

My fourth grade teacher, Herr Brunner, was a well-built, handsome man with a red beard and glittering, intense dark eyes. His lessons were interesting, but he would rap a student hard on her hand when she did not obey or did not do her homework. The culprit had to go to his desk and hold out her hand, and he slapped her hard with his ruler. Sometimes big welts would appear on her hand. We alternately loved or hated him, but always admired him. His nickname was Lohengrin, because he resembled the stage hero of Wagner's opera with his red beard and manly stature. But he was a sick man, and later had to go to prison for taking liberties with one of his students.

At the end of fourth grade, all students in Germany and most other European countries had to take a vital test that would determine their futures. The children who failed this test had to stay in the elementary school, which gave them eight grades of basic education and prepared them for lives as factory workers, craftsmen, waitresses, salesgirls or other lower-class occupations. There were few opportunities for further advancement after eighth grade, yet the young people had a chance to go to an academic school that would end with the abitur, the entrance exam for the university.

Most of the fourteen-year-olds took apprentice jobs, but continued to go one afternoon a week to a school where they could take general education or occupational education classes.

The students who passed the fourth grade test were allowed to go on to secondary school. In Nuernberg, and I think throughout the country, tuition was necessary for secondary school which continued to the 10th grade, and the middle class students usually went on to study in secondary school, while the more intelligent students of the working class continued in elementary school because their parents could not afford the tuition and few scholarships were given to them. There was another exception to this rule. If the child of wealthy parents flunked the crucial test, he or she could always continue in a private secondary school, where the curriculum was easy, but without the stigma of public elementary school.

All of the girls in our private preparatory school passed the test with flying colors and proceeded as students in the municipal girls' Lyceum, a school that taught modern languages, science and math, and ended with a test after tenth grade. The test was still called, colloquially, "Das Einjaehrige," the one year test, because, in the old Reich, boys had to serve in the military for three years after they finished elementary school, but only for one year if they graduated from tenth grade.

In the Lyceum, we had different teachers for each subject, but we remained in our classroom while the teachers moved from class to class. Only for physical education, music, needlework and art did we have special classrooms, and in the higher grades we had a science room. Our schedule was very complicated because we had to study so many different subjects, some once, some twice, some three or four periods per week.

For religion, the whole class would split up. Nuernberg is a predominantly Protestant city, and two of the three sections of our class were entirely Protestant. The population was 33 percent Catholic, but only five of the approximately 90 students in each grade were Catholic because most of the Catholic students went to parochial schools. Only 2½% of the population of Nuernberg was Jewish, but at least 15% of the students in the secondary schools were Jewish because most Jewish families belonged to the middle class and put a high value on education. The Jewish Orthodox congregation, which had many members who had come from Poland and Russia, and who belonged to the lower class, had a Jewish elementary school, which had a more demanding program than the public elementary schools, and taught English along with occupational courses.

We went to school six days a week from eight in the morning to one o'clock in the afternoon. This was in 1921, when we lived the year round on the Ludwigshoehe. The morning train to town left at 7:07 a.m. We waited many mornings in the bitterly cold, unheated waiting room, stomping around in an effort to keep warm, while our breath formed dense clouds of steam when we exhaled. When the train got stuck in the snow and was late, even Papa waited with us at the station. But, usually, he left the house after seven and ran downhill all the way to the train station until he jumped on the already departing train, which often waited patiently for his arrival. Sometimes he missed the train and had to walk one and half miles to meet the later train that did not stop at our small community.

Floh took the 12:17 train home that stopped at the Ludwigshoehe, but my schedule ended at 1:00. I had to take the 1:58 train that did not stop there. I had to wait sitting on the train with other commuting students for nearly one hour before it left. I did not mind that at all because the Orient Express stopped for five minutes on the same platform as the train in which we waited. We watched the luxury train with its interesting passengers, and dreamed of being on their train to go to the far away countries of the East. I also was busy reading the textbooks of the older students on the train. The best part of going home on the late train was my boyfriend Heini Bollendorf, whose hair was as flaming red as mine, and whose face was even more freckled than mine.

Heini lived not far from our house and we had a long uphill walk of one and a half miles from the train station with a rest stop at the brook on the edge of the forest. Sometimes a peasant offered us a ride on his cow-drawn wagon, but we usually declined, feeling sorry for the poor beast. Heini used to carry my books, and when it was cold or rainy we huddled close together and walked arm in arm.

When I came home around 3:00, a stale, warmed-up lunch waited for me. I was tired and worn out after lunch, but my mother insisted that I do my homework, before I was allowed to go out and play. Mama used to sit opposite me at the desk in the alcove, where she had her sewing drawer, and she supervised me, sewing or mending stockings while I did my homework. At that time, children had to write with steel pens dipped in ink, and with my poor coordination I covered my writing with many nasty inkblots. When Mama saw my sloppy work, she tore it up and I had to start it all over again. This usually continued until my paper was covered with bitter tears, besides the blots. It often took several hours before I was able to produce an acceptable paper and was allowed to play.

In her later years, Mama was full of remorse for torturing me with her sadistic games, and begged me for forgiveness. By that time my frustrations were forgotten, and I had learned a lesson from her: never give up before my work was satisfactory to myself.

As soon as I was allowed to leave the house, I ran over to Heini's house to play in his garden, and to take a dip in his swimming hole. One day, I stepped into a nest of ground wasps while leaving the water. I screamed with pain, and my foot swelled to enormous proportions. I had to stay at home for the rest of the week with soothing compresses on my foot. I lay on the sofa and read to my heart's content, happy not to have to write any homework.

The Sunday before returning to school after my absence, I picked wild flowers, one bouquet for each of my teachers. When I entered the train, still a little clumsy on my foot, my hands full of flowers, somebody slammed the door of the coach on my hand. I had to return home on the next train and was forced to stay home for another two days, this time with the compresses on my swollen hand.

Floh and I usually rode in the second-last coach from the rear of the train, where we met a group of Jewish friends who came from Huettenbach, three stations further in the hills, which had a large Jewish population.

They were all older than we were, but we developed a rewarding friendship. My special friend was Hugo Burkhard, a young businessman who told me that he would marry me when I grew up, and who, while on business trips, wrote beautiful postcards to his little "bride."

I lost track of Hugo in later years but found a book authored by him about his horrifying years in concentration camps during the war. Through his book I learned about the fate of many of our friends who were in the same camps.

XIV. Nuernberg Again

In fall 1922, we moved back to Nuernberg into our old apartment in the Fuertherstrasse that had been sublet and was still in our name because Mama was afraid that the daily commuting would be too much for our little boys, who would soon be ready for school, and grandmother was now too old to be bothered with boarders. Mama also hoped that she could enjoy more of her husband's company when he did not have to lose time commuting.

That hope was not realized. Instead of coming home according to the train schedule, Papa would work long hours of overtime in the business, was late for lunch, and seldom showed up for dinner. This cost Mama torrents of tears and during the next few years she developed ulcers that kept her in bed much of the time.

One ray of joy was the new automobile. It was an antique car called a Thuricum. It was made in Switzerland and looked much like an early Model-A Ford. Papa was the only one in the family to acquire a driver's license, and many Sundays we went to visit customers, to buy wood for the factory, or to visit relatives. Papa also made several longer business trips in the car. Mama was always eager to come along, blissfully happy when her wish was granted, uncontrollably depressed when she was left behind.

Fritz was the saddest loser in the move. We gave him to neighbors, but when we came after a few weeks to visit him, we found the poor dog chained and despondent. He rallied a bit when he saw us, and begged us with all the means of expression at his disposal to take him along with us. This we did. We took him to Nuernberg, where he could stay at the stable with Herr Schuemel, the stablemaster, where we could visit him from time to time. But here, also, he had to be chained most of the time, and he missed the forest even more than we did. When we were later able to keep him at home again he had lost his spirit and joy. He became blind, but lived out his life in sedate gratitude to be home again.

I was very depressed during the first months after our return to Nuernberg. To cheer me up, Papa brought home from the store the furniture for a daughter's room, putting it in my room on the condition that he could show it to customers on request. This led to many arguments because I was sloppy and the room was often in disorder when Papa came to show it off.

The furniture of this room was really spectacular, and it became a bestseller in the store. It consisted of a bed, a desk that opened up into a vanity, a wardrobe, and a large bookcase with matching table and chairs. The furniture was painted in a gay green with silhouettes of birds and flowers. It was put in our former guestroom, and a sofa bed for overnight guests completed the outfit. I did not have enough books for the large bookcase, but I had inherited from aunt Ada her "museum," a collection of miniatures of everything under the sun that could be made into miniatures--pottery, dolls, trees, plants, houses, tiny pieces of furniture and so on. I continued to add little pieces to the collection, and displayed my museum with pride to friends and visitors.

I had one great friendship during sixth and the beginning of seventh grade, my friend Lenchen Scherer, a petite blonde with blue eyes, pigtails and rosy cheeks like a doll. Lenchen lived only one block from our house in the same street, but her house was in a different neighborhood from our block of fashionable apartments. The block where she lived had nothing but coldwater tenements.

Her father was a streetcar conductor, and they were poor in comparison with the people I had known thus far in my life. She was the recipient of a scholarship, while the rest of the class had to pay tuition and came from the wealthy middle class.

Her apartment was much smaller than ours. Her two older brothers slept on couches in the seldom-used parlor. Lenchen and her younger sister shared a bed in a kitchen that also served as a living room, and in which the family took their weekly bath because the washroom contained only the commode and a tiny cold-water sink. Only the parents had their own bedroom. But, nevertheless, as was typical, they had a "gute Stube," an unheated parlor that was never used except for special occasions. Lenchen and I played in this room with our dolls, often shivering from the cold, but happy to be undisturbed in our make-believe world, for which we were really too old but which we two immature girls still needed.

The kitchen was always warm from the range and the kindness of Lenchen's overworked mother, who sat at the large table with work in her hands, mending, sewing, cleaning vegetables, or ironing, while we did our homework in heavenly peace, away from Mama's interference. Lenchen had to work hard to keep her grades up to qualify for the scholarship, while learning came easy for me. My grades were quite good, and Mama was eventually content not to supervise my homework, because she was either sick, went to the movies, visited her mother and friends, or entertained at home.

My Ludwig cousins lived at that time in Zirndorf, a little town near Fuerth where Hans conducted his business in furniture accessories, and where the girls went to school. We did not see them very often during the school year. Only during the summer vacations did we spend time in Zirndorf, and one or the other of them used the sofabed in my room. Elvira and I had a wonderful pastime when she visited us. We played often in the exhibition rooms of the furniture store, and it was our special delight to pose as mannequins in the fully furnished rooms in the many show windows. We sat motionless in the windows where people collected, debating whether we were dolls or real, until we made faces at them. Unfortunately, our elders got wise to our unbecoming conduct and chased us away.

We were only just installed in our new surroundings and Papa was on one of his frequent trips to Holland when tragedy struck. Papa's older brother, Adolf, who lived next door to us, got sick with a general infection. There was no penicillin in those days and the doctors and family stood helpless as he died within three days. Mama had no way to get in touch with Papa, and had to tell him the bad news when she met him at the railway station.

From then on Papa had to neglect his successful export business because he had to take Adolf's place in the retail store. Times were not good for business. Papa spent a lot of money on advertising. His older brother Issi, a cautious, timid man, was appalled by the expenses. Adolf's son Fred and Issi's son Alex who were also in the family business resented Papa's leadership, and they ganged up on him. Mama saw little of her beloved Arthur, and when she saw him he was nervous and tired. It was a bad year for both of them. But 1923 was even worse.

Since the end of the war, we had had a creeping inflation in Germany. Everything got more and more expensive. In 1923 inflation got completely out of hand, an effect of the Versailles Treaty. However, the theory that Hitler proposed was that a conspiracy of international Jewry caused the runaway inflation, and it was the one accepted by a great part of the population. It was repeated and hammered into the heads of the Germans during every election. It was one of the reasons that Germans so readily accepted Hitler's slogan, "The Jews are our misfortune." There were many elections during the next ten years, and every election brought a shift to the right.

People talked about nothing else but the runaway inflation but I was so busy with my tasks of childhood that I was not personally involved until one day my mother gave me a bill of one million marks, a one with six zeros, and told me to go to the store and buy a dozen eggs. After the saleslady had wrapped up my eggs, I gave her my bill. The lady shook her head and said, "Eggs are two million today."

I returned home for the additional money, and thereafter asked many questions about the inflation.

The inflation brought changes in Germany's social structure. The poor remained as poor as they had been before. At the time of the inflation, unemployment was no great problem because whoever had money invested it immediately in nonperishable goods, and people from other countries imported German goods which they could buy at bargain prices with their stable money. U.S. dollars were highly priced because they did not lose their value. But it was hard for the workers because they had to spend their wages within hours after receiving them, to get full value. Workers were paid twice weekly, and eventually even daily.

People who lived on the income from their money, or were pensioned, lost their last penny. I remember that I had a savings account into which, for years, I had paid all my birthday money and other monetary gifts. This account was reduced to nothing. To pay their grocery bills, many people had to sell their heirlooms, works of art, jewelry and antique furniture, which were gobbled up by the newly rich who had profited by the inflation. People who were in debt, or were paying off their mortgages, could pay them with worthless paper money, and suddenly became rich. Many businesses went bankrupt, and the people who bought their shops and factories became rich.

Papa stopped his sales campaign and sold only enough to cover day-to-day expenses while increasing his stock, much against the advice of his brother and nephews. They did not become rich, but had their business intact after the money stabilization.

Farmers and people whose income was derived from their special knowledge and skills, such as doctors, lawyers, teachers and craftsmen, neither gained nor lost much, and after years of difficulties could pick up their lives where they had been before the disaster. However, profiteers who bought valuable goods for valueless money amassed great fortunes, and became the class of the newly rich. They indulged in conspicuous consumption, and in spite of their lack of education, invaded the upper class.

Title page of an edition of Der Stuermer in May, 1937.

XV. My First Encounter With Evil

When my mother suggested that I start piano lessons with Julie Fischer, a former friend of Aunt Ada's, I was delighted. I liked Julie and I liked music. I could already peck out the melodies of all the songs I knew on the piano, and I played the harmonica. I had a clear and true voice, although not as pleasing as Emilie's or her daughters.

But, musically, things did not turn out well for me. With my clumsy hands and lack of coordination, I could not combine left and right hands. I practiced and practiced, at first voluntarily, later forced by my mother, and more and more unwilling, but without success. I was always scolded for my laziness and lack of cooperation. It was deeply depressing for me that pupils who had started at the same time as I did could play the nicest pieces of music, while I struggled with scales, boring etudes, and simple pieces of music written for beginners.

In 1923, I also had my first glimpse of anti-Semitism. My piano teacher was then in a different part of town. It was a 45-minute walk. My mother always gave me fare for the streetcar. I usually took the streetcar going there, but I would usually walk home either along the beautiful promenade which surrounded the old city walls with a narrow park, or through the narrow lanes of the old city with its medieval houses and churches.

In one of the old buildings, a triangular house where two streets formed a fork, Julius Streicher, the infamous Nazi, published his notorious hate sheet, a pornographic and sadistic weekly magazine with the motto, "The Jews are our Misfortune." Under blazing headlines like "Unspeakable Crimes of a True Student of the Talmud," or "Jewish Incest," or "A German Virgin in the Hands of Her Jewish Doctor," he showed repulsive cartoons of Jews with huge, beaked noses and thick lips, and wrote about their alleged crimes.

The name of the paper was "Der Stuermer," The Assailant. In it, Streicher created the myth that the inflation was a scheme of the Jews to take away the wealth of the Germans and collect it in their own hands, a myth that was widely accepted as true. He also tried to show that Germany's defeat in World War I was the result of manipulations by the Jews.

However, his compulsive preoccupation was the sex life of Jewish men. According to him, the all-encompassing goal of Jewish men, after their lust for money, was the undermining of German morals by seducing or raping innocent, blonde, blue-eyed German virgins.

Every week, the newest edition of Der Stuermer was displayed in glass cases on both fronts of the house. A crowd of people always stood there, avidly reading the repetitious trash. I stood among them on my way home from my piano lesson, afraid that they would find out that I was one of the depraved race, deeply ashamed of the crimes my people were accused of, and strangely excited by the lurid, lewd tales.

What I did not know at that time was that the "poor, innocent maidens" enjoyed the fun in bed, as well as the generous, lavish presents from their Jewish lovers, and, far from being seduced, preferred them to their miserly Aryan boy friends. I also did not know that most men of that period in Europe thought that men were polygamous by nature, and believed that extramarital diversions were necessary for the good of their health. While middle-class girls were encouraged to remain virgins until they married, it was considered inevitable for a boy to utilize his manhood as soon as it bothered him.

Standing there in the crowd, looking at the frightful cartoons and reading the atrocious stories, I felt guilty and miserable, while desperately munching the candy I had bought with the money I had not spent on car fare. This was my first encounter with anti-semitism.

Throughout the Twenties, political strife was the order of the day. Huge posters invited people to attend political rallies, whether it was Communists, the Nazis, or the more moderate of the numerous political parties. Nazi posters always had the underlined warning: Jews not admitted.

We children were also involved in politics by our graffiti campaign. Youngsters scrawled hammers and sickles, or swastikas, with chalk or paint on sidewalks, walls, or on the fronts of houses. Children whose parents were social democrats, democrats, or Jewish, were also armed with chalk that they had taken clandestinely from school. They changed swastikas into squares, or hanged them from gallows.

XVI. The Youth Movement

Towards the end of the nineteenth century, a small group of high school students in a small German town formed a club which started a movement that spread like wildfire throughout Germany and affected the lives of most young people in Germany during the early twentieth century.

The movement was called the "Wandervogel," the "wandering bird." Its philosophy attracted the best of young men with its ideals of purity, idealism, and simplicity. It was a revolt against the hypocritical bourgeoisie of the German middle class. Its members, like the hippies in America later, let their hair grow long. They wore simple, distinctive clothes and sandals. They hiked through the forests and mountains, slept in barns or simple tents, and cooked their own food. They collected folk songs and stories from the peasants of their area. They accompanied themselves on the guitar. They shunned social dancing, replacing it with old German square dances. They played ball games and revived old sports, such as lance throwing. Unlike the hippies, they avoided drugs, drinking, smoking, and illicit sex.

At the beginning it was a strictly male association that chose its leaders from its own ranks, rejecting adult leadership. They were in opposition to the Boy Scouts, with its rituals, adult leadership, and emphasis on achievement.

While the hippies were united by their disapproval of an unnecessary war, the members of the Wandervogel were united by a deep love for their country and nature. During World War I, many of them volunteered for service in the army long before their age group was called up, and many of them lost their lives in combat.

The organization of the Wandervogel survived the war, but during the political strife after the war they broke up into many splinter groups, some joining the national, patriotic, and anti-republican parties, others becoming the youth groups of the socialist and communist parties. Hitler recruited many of them into his Hitler Youth, and the communists found in them the nucleus of their youth organization, Spartacus. Girls finally also organized youth groups, among them the rightist Bund Deutscher Maedschen, the Alliance of German girls. Eventually, coed groups were formed and flourished.

Since the patriotic youth organizations did not accept Jewish members, separate Jewish groups were formed and they joined the confusing array of longhaired groups that hiked through the countryside, singing, marching, playing the guitar and sleeping in the newly formed youth hostels.

Floh and I joined the Kameraden, the German Jewish hiking group, in 1923. The Blau-Weiss, the Blue-White, another Jewish group, was Zionistic. They had all the patriotism and idealism of other youth groups, but their patriotism was directed towards Zion, the future Jewish state. Our parents, German patriots who believed in a future for Jews in Germany, discouraged us from joining the Blau-Weiss. The ideals of Kameraden, which were full assimilation into German culture and society without losing sight of our Jewish heritage, were more in line with their ideology. Ours was an impossible dream, because the German nationalists hated and feared the Jews, and accepted them only if they gave up their Jewishness.

Nevertheless, we imitated the lifestyle of the Wandervogel. We adopted their songs and folk dances, their hiking rituals, their weekly meetings of reading (mostly Hermann Hesse and Rainer Maria Rilke), singing, playing guitars, and discussion in small groups, as well as their aversion to alcohol, smoking, and sex.

My den mother was Rita Gans, a distant cousin, and on Sundays we met together with all the other Kameraden to go for a hike. We met, like numerous other groups of young people, at 7 a.m. at the railway station. Our traditional meeting place was "under the tail," the tail on a statue of the Bavarian king on horseback. We took one of the special Sunday morning trains to the foothills of the Franconian Swiss, where we hiked, marched, or played ball in the lovely forests and mountains, brooks and meadows, passing quaint villages and little castles or ruins on the way.

Since my piano teacher also played the guitar, I was finally able to give up my piano lessons, and instead learned to play the guitar, which was easy for me because I could pick out the chords of nearly every tune I heard once.

I was a member of the Kameraden for many years, and so were my three brothers. Once, we had a national meeting in a village not far from Nuernberg. I was still very young, and could not understand the painful discussions of our leaders who already felt that we would never be able to obtain our ideals. One group splintered off to join the socialistic movement, others asked for more involvement in Jewish problems, while others tended to isolate themselves in an ivory tower of aloofness and idealism.

For us young ones, the romance of sleeping in the hay in a barn, dancing around the midsummer night's bonfire, and singing together with groups from all over Germany was enough to keep us busy and happy without sharing the dilemma of our elders. I later became a den mother myself, and my little charges had a crush on me and were jealous of each other when I taught some of them to strum the guitar. But during my later years with the Kameraden, I remained on the periphery, without deep bonds to the other members, and without believing in their ideal that Jews could enter into the mainstream of German culture.

Eventually, I was kicked out of the Kameraden because I became a society girl who flirted, participated in ballroom dancing, drinking and smoking.

The Stoewer

XVII. Transportation And The Factory

I have already written about our elegant horsedrawn coach, and our first car, the Thurikum, a car similar to a Model-A Ford that was lit by carbide lamps. These lamps gave off a weak glimmer that could be seen by oncoming traffic, but did not light the road, which made night driving a nightmare, especially when we were with Papa, who was night blind. We always planned our trips so that we would arrive home in daylight. But, more often than not, we had a flat, and it took Papa the better part of an hour to change the tire. Then we had to crawl along at ten miles an hour in the darkness, and usually landed on the shoulder of the road or even in a ditch. Once we had to stay overnight in a hotel less than 20 miles from Nuernberg.

The Thurikum was very drab looking even in those early years, and was later exchanged for a posh Stoewer convertible. Because the Thurikum looked so shabby, we had it to ourselves most of the time, but the elegant Stoewer that replaced the old car belonged to the business and was shared by the three Braun families. As my cousins got their own driver's licenses, we rarely used it anymore.

By 1926, we were completely without any car. Papa was sick and tired of the daily differences with his brother and nephews. He also was afraid for his own sons, who would have to work with their much older cousins when they were ready to enter the business. So he left the furniture store to the other Braun families and kept the neglected furniture factory in Fuerth for himself.

The factory was about 10 miles from our house, and Papa was too impatient to use public transportation. Money for a new car was not available when he had to invest and reinvest in the factory, so he bought himself a motorcycle. He enjoyed it very much, but Mama was disappointed because she was too heavy and clumsy to ride on the back seat.

We children were happy to ride with Papa one at a time, though he spilled us quite often, always cautioning before a fall, "Vorsicht, Stefferle, wir fallen." (Be careful, Steffi, we are going to fall.) I got bruised, but continued to ride with Papa whenever he invited me.

He liked to take me along when he went to one or the other of the sawmills in the vicinity to buy wood. Our factory made furniture from plywood, laminated with a thin layer of precious hardwood showing an interesting grain. I helped him choose hardwood that would make interesting patterns. Houses in Germany were built with few or no closets, and the most important feature of the bedroom was the huge wardrobe. The doors of this wardrobe were decorated with intricate patterns of thin layers of hardwood. I became an expert in wood and in furniture making. The boys were still too young to show great interest in Papa's work, while I loved to spend time in the factory, and Papa was proud to explain every step in the production. We had about 100 workers, most of them expert carpenters. Papa believed that he had a mission to introduce modern furniture with clean simple lines and expanses of highly polished, interesting hardwood patterns. Though he had had little formal schooling, he had natural good taste, and had taught himself the history of art.

It was a great pleasure to visit a museum, an art exhibition, a cathedral or a castle with him. He was a great teacher, and I was his adoring student.

Papa often traveled by motorbike or train to other cities to sell his furniture, and Mama nagged and nagged about being left behind. At last Papa bought a heavy motorcycle with a sidecar where she could ride, often together with one of the boys, while I sat proudly on the back seat. We visited not only sawmills but relatives that lived in small villages through Franconia and Wurtemberg.

Papa had a distant cousin, Karl, who had married a rich woman. During the inflation, he speculated with her money, became very wealthy, and was now a member of the much despised class of the "Newly Rich." He loved to show off his new affluence, and looked down on us as his poor relatives.

Karl and his wife had a beautiful daughter, Latte, a spoiled brat with barely any brains.

One Sunday, Papa decided that it was time to visit his sister Babette in Gunzenhausen, a little town 50 miles south of Nuernberg. Babette was a widow, bedridden with terminal cancer, whose children tended her little grocery store. On our way there, Karl overtook us and invited me to ride with them in their elegant Mercedes, since he was also going to visit Aunt Babette. I went with them but got bored with their conversation about all the expensive clothes and furniture they had bought, and about their new villa and their wonderful car. Karl, himself, did not drive, but had a liveried chauffeur. While Karl and his wife visited Aunt Babette upstairs, Latte and I waited in the little grocery store, where our cousins, whom we barely knew, fed us almonds and raisins from the store. Finally, my parents arrived. Karl invited me to continue with them and have lunch, but I declined. Mama and Papa did not let me visit Aunt Babette, whom I barely knew, because she was too sick.

We left soon, had a picnic lunch by the wayside, and continued on our way. As we drove leisurely through the countryside, the tire fell off the wheel of the sidecar and rolled far into a wheat field while the sidecar continued to rattle along on the rim of the wheel, frightening Mama until she screamed. Nobody was hurt, but Papa could not put the tire back on the bent wheel. A crowd of children on bikes collected around the scene of the accident and retrieved the wayward tire.

We needed help, and I suggested that I borrow a bike from one of the boys to go to the next town for a tow truck. I don't remember why I went instead of one of the children, but I rode off just as Karl and family passed by and offered me a ride in his car. Remembering how bored I had been with them in the morning, I declined their offer.

I had never ridden a boy's bike before, and all went well until I came to a steep hill. The brakes failed, and I crashed full force into a telephone pole, smashing the borrowed bike, and cutting a deep hole in my knee.

Karl, who had stood and chatted with my parents, caught up with me and found me lying in the street. He arranged for a tow truck, his wife bandaged my bleeding knee, and I had to ride home with them. My parents stayed overnight in the little town and settled with the boy for the ruined bike. The sidecar could not be repaired right away. Mama and the sidecar had to go home on the train, and Papa rode the motorcycle without the sidecar.

I ran around for a while with the bandaged knee, and as soon as I could ride my bike again, I got caught in the streetcar tracks, fell on barely healed knee, limped for the rest of the summer, and could not even go swimming with the heavily bandaged knee.

Papa ended up with a kidney ailment resulting from either the draft on the bike or its vibrations. He went to a spa with healing waters for diseases of the kidney, where he flirted with every available female. He even sent us a postcard of himself with a beautiful woman whom he met at the spa. Mama cried her heart out with jealousy at home and made us all miserable.

When Papa returned home, he sold the motorcycle. He bought a tiny electrical car with an accumulator that had to be charged every night. This tiny vehicle could go only 20 miles per hour, and could seat only two people. The bright side of it was that one did not need a driver's license to drive it, and I proudly drove it to Fuerth with my father in the back seat.

In 1929 we finally bought a car of our own. It was an NSU which seated four people. By squeezing together and putting a tiny stool on the floor, all six of us could be fitted in. Riding in the NSU was a great way to bring the family close together at a time when all of us went our own ways, and the infrequent Sunday outings were the only time the family was united. That car was later taken away by the Nazis and, after the war, when my father came back to Germany, it was still around and was given back to him, and he finally sold it.

The N.S.U.

In the orchard. Papa, Werner, Grandmother Emilie, Heinz, Floh, Steffi and Hedwig.

XVIII. New House, New School, New Friends

In 1924, the family business flourished thanks to Papa's foresight in increasing the stock of furniture during the year of runaway inflation. He felt that he deserved a reward in spite of the daily fights with his brother and nephews about the conduct of the business.

Our apartment in the Fuertherstrasse was dark and damp, and too small for growing children. Mama and Lily had a new pastime, house hunting. Finally, they found a house and garden that they thought was ideal for us. It was very expensive, situated in the fashionable northern part of the city, the Kobergerstrasse, and after Papa, Toni and Hede had seen it, they rented it, and we soon moved there.

It was an old Victorian sandstone villa. We were not the only renters. Sandwiched between our living quarters on the second and third floor, and the kitchen in the basement, an old woman was living with her widowed daughter. We had to pass through their hall on the way from our upper rooms to our kitchen and utility room. Fortunately, a dumbwaiter had been installed between the kitchen and the upstairs hall, the shaft of which served also for communication between upstairs and downstairs. When our noise grew too loud, the old lady would appear in the hall, shouting at us, but she was half deaf, and only excessive noise disturbed her.

Maria went downstairs from her third floor bedroom in the morning and did not use the stairs again until she was done with her work, but the maid had to run up and down stairs all day long, always muttering and complaining. Whenever she ran across one of us children, she found a reason to scold us, and her shrieks were heard all through the house.

The rooms on the second floor were large and high ceilinged, which created a heating problem. Only the living room was heated. The beautiful white glazed tile oven gave a pleasant warmth and warm water to wash ourselves. We had to carry the hot water to the upstairs bathroom and share it, which often left us with a dirty neck or black fingernails. The gas heater in the bathroom was only used on Saturday for the weekly ritual of a warm bath. Even then we had to economize, and the three boys had to share one bathtub full of water. The water was usually so dirty that they called me in to keep them company, without fear that I might have a glimpse of their naked bodies.

The bathroom was large, and had many wardrobes. It also had a mysterious door near the outside corner. This door was locked when we rented the house. We had a key made for it, and finally explored what was behind it. We found a winding staircase that led to a room in a turret that was furnished as a monk's cell, complete with a life size statue of a monk in a moth-eaten habit, wooden bread, and wooden mice who were nibbling at the wooden bread. It was utterly trashy, and we children loved it dearly.

The kitchen was the size of a ballroom, and caused Maria much harm, because she had to traverse its hard cement floor with tired feet. Her disposition grew more and more quarrelsome as years went by, but her friendship with Mama and her allegiance to the family remained undiminished.

Next to the house was a large, neglected garden, planted only with grass, bushes and trees. In the garden stood an unused greenhouse with broken panes, a toolshed, and a garden house with a round table and benches where the Kameraden were allowed to meet. Best of all, there was a doghouse in the garden, where Fritz lived out his later years in peace, surrounded by friendship.

A large, neglected park, a children's paradise, with gazebos, broken plaster statues, crumbling, dry fountains, and lush, uncontrolled underbrush, also belonged to the property.

During our first summer in Kobergerstrasse, we children used this park constantly, enacting the most romantic dramas, but to save on the rent we did not renew our lease on this part of the property at the end of the first year.

Mama wrote in her diary during those years, "Our expenses, and the way we have arranged our household, are much too high. I feel responsible for this, without having the means and ways to change it. We always say 'If we could only afford to live the way we do.' "

The river Pegnitz divides Nuernberg into two parts. At the time I lived there, each side was called after its parish church, St. Lorenz or St. Sebaldus. We lived on the St.Lorenz side, and since the train station was also on that side, I first went to school there. Our new house was on the Sebaldus side of the river, and I had to change schools. It was the same type of school, and was frequented by girls from the middle class.

I was well accepted in my new school, but my greatest joy was that I made a new friend, Ilse Jaeger, who was commuting every day from the Ludwigshoehe. She should have gone to my old school, but she had a friend in our school, and therefore preferred the long walk to school from the train station in order to have at least one friend in the new school. Though Ilse was not Jewish, her friends were mostly Jewish. She was full of laughter and fun, a beautiful girl with blonde pigtails and blue eyes. Besides Dorle Bing, who knew her before she came to us, three of us became her inseparable friends, a Christian girl Frieda Harrer, Hanni Nussbaum and I. The five of us spent every break together in the schoolyard.

Frieda joined us when we formed a group to have tennis lessons together on two afternoons in summer. Again, I was handicapped because of my lack of coordination, but I bravely continued though the others beat me at most of the games. Hanni did not join us for the tennis lessons, because her family was too poor to pay the expense.

My school in the Labenwolfstrasse.

Hanni's father was a Jewish tailor who had come from Russia.
Hanni's mother had died young, and her father had remarried
a woman who could never get close to her three step-
daughters. She became ill--I think she had diabetes--and had a
leg amputated. She lay all day in the living room or in her
bedroom in the dark and frugal apartment where they lived,
and where Mr. Nussbaum had his workshop. Though she was
Jewish, Hanni did not go with the rest of us to Jewish instruction. Her father belonged to the Jewish Orthodox Congregation. Hanni did not go to their instructions either, because
she considered herself an atheist.

She belonged to the Zionistic youth organization Blau-Weiss. She invited Dorle and me to join her on their trips to Wendelstein, where the Blau-Weiss had a little house, built by the members themselves, who prepared themselves for a life in Palestine--or Erez Israel as we called it before it became the state of Israel--by learning manual labor. Our parents disapproved of our connection with the "Ostjuden," Jews who came from Poland or Russia, and who generally did not belong to the upper-middle class. So we did not join her club, but continued our friendship with her. Hanni was more independent than we were, and she was a smart but not outstanding student. She had a wonderful, dark complexion, and dark, straight hair, but her mouth and nose were too large for her small, delicate face to be pretty.

We often went together on hiking and bike tours, more often than not to the Ludwigshoehe, where we stayed in Ilse's house or in our orchard. As time went by, I visited Ilse more often in the Ludwigshoehe than the other friends did, and was a frequent house guest, and Ilse slept often on my sofa-bed after we went to the opera, a concert, or a play.

Dorle, Ilse, Hanni and I decided to take a one-week hiking trip during the Easter vacation in 1925, while we were 13 and 14 years old. Our parents had no objections to the tour, as long as an older girl came along as a chaperone. I had a friend, Gabriele, from the Kameraden in Bamberg, the Bishop's See, 50 miles north of Nuernberg. I called her and she agreed to be our chaperone.

Easter was late that year, and on Palm Sunday we packed our knapsacks and took the train to Bamberg. The weather was warm and sunny. I had gotten my first camera on my last birthday, and the trip is well documented. It was an unforgettable event in our lives because it was the first time that we were completely on our own.

Gabriele, our chaperone, was the daughter of a rich banker. We were not prepared for all the pomp and circumstance that awaited us in her house. A butler opened the door and led us to a lavishly furnished salon. It was huge, with deep carpets, ornate draperies, Louis Quatorze furniture and original oil paintings on the walls. We did not dare to sit down and just looked around, intimidated, while waiting for Gabriele. She finally appeared, dressed in a simple hiking outfit, with her knapsack packed, ready to accompany us--but only for two days.

We were quite disappointed but set out to take the train to the beautiful valley of the Main River. We stopped at a place where a famous baroque church stood on a hill overlooking the valley. It was a church that was frequented by pilgrims, and a fair, selling articles for the faithful, was in front of the church.

The church was called Vierzehnheiligen, ("Fourteen Saints") because it was consecrated to fourteen saints. The inside was all in white and gold, with many ornaments, statues, and pictures that created a gay, festive mood. After we had admired the church, we went to a meadow where we had a cookout of burnt cereal that we ate heroically under the bare trees in the chilly afternoon. A friar joined us, and was very astonished that four of us were Jewish girls. Gabriele had brought a fancy cake and a bottle of sweet wine, a rare treat, and a blessing after our miserable meal. The friar joined us in the feast, and we were amazed that he was a human being under his, for us unaccustomed, habit.

We spent the night in a youth hostel in the valley, and took the train the next morning to Koburg, an old town near the northern border of Bavaria. We registered at the youth hostel there and then went sightseeing in the narrow streets of the old medieval town. The rest of the day we spent in the old castle. I remember us, as we sat on the parapet, looking down into the valley, playing out games in which we were knights and dames at a tournament. We laughed and giggled all the time, and people passing us stood and smiled at our good humor.

When it was time for Gabriele to leave us, we had already decided to go on without her and face the wrath of our parents when we came home.

We set out northward the next morning into the beautiful hills of the Thuringian Forest. We wandered for a long time and our feet began to hurt, but we had to go on to the next town with a youth hostel. We tried to hitchhike, but none of the cars stopped for us until a funny contraption came along. It was a truck on which stood a beautiful carriage, like our old carriage. It had a coat of arms painted on its side. The driver told us to sit in the carriage, which we did with immense pleasure. We sat in splendor, waving graciously at the people on the road until the rain started. The driver then pulled a canvas over the coach, and we sat in darkness, telling each other ghost stories until we reached our destination, a little town named Sonnenberg, a center of glassblowing and dollmaking. We slept again in the youth hostel, and visited a toy factory and a glassblower's shop where artificial eyes were made. We hiked another day across the mountains and came to a place with a very small and primitive hostel. We were the only guests, except for a young man whom we nicknamed Gabriel, after our lost chaperone. Then we took the train back to Bamberg, because we had had no time to visit the famous Cathedral of Bamberg on our way north, and we wanted to visit it now.

The cathedral was begun in the early Middle Ages in solid Romantic style, and was finished many centuries later as a gothic cathedral. It contains many medieval works of art, but we girls were most impressed by the solemn mood and the scent of incense that pervaded the immense building.

When we took the train back home, we were completely exhausted from our tour, and all four of us fell asleep until we reached Nuernberg, where our parents received us without any reproaches.

XIX. Last Years of Childhood

While we were living in the Fuertherstrasse, we often visited grandmother, because she lived between our home and our school, but after our move to the Kobergerstrasse we saw less and less of her. We children were busy with our new schools and our garden. Grandmother lived far away, and did not come to visit us anymore. I think our mother did not want us to see much of Grandmother during her final years because of her deterioration and regression into her former, self-destructive personality.

When grandmother died, she was not quite 67 years old. Mama wrote in her diary, "Mother died in January 1925. Her last years were sad, bitter, and dissatisfied. The difficult life, and her progressive illness, made it nearly impossible to communicate with her. It was a pity that we could not cheer up her last years. It was impossible because of her unfortunate disposition. Hede had to suffer most, because she had to live with and care for her, and suffered under her ill temper. I barely dare say it, it sounds so cruel, but her death was a blessing to her. Unfortunately, Hede is now suffering from arthritis, otherwise, she could be happy and carefree."

Hede kept part of her apartment, and sublet the rest of it to nice people. She often came to visit now, and loved to play rummy and other simple card games with us.

The three sisters divided grandmother's possessions. Toni got the dinner service and the hand-painted china by David Ottensooser, mother got the beautifully hand-painted coffee service, bed and table linen, and Hede got the furniture and family silver.

To their own surprise, the division of grandmother's household goods did not cause any friction between the three sisters but, on other occasions, all three of them quarreled often and noisily. The final insult they hurled at each other was always, "You are exactly like your mother!"

Later that year the apartment Toni and Heinz had sublet in Berlin Friedenau became vacant and they moved back to Berlin. When they moved back they found that the old apartment was too small for them. They divided the girls' bedroom with a curtain to create a tiny office, and the hall was crowded with shelves of merchandise.

Elfriede and Elvira fell in love with their new school in Berlin. The school had high academic standards, but the joy of the Ludwig girls was the physical education department. They all enjoyed gymnastics and being on the rowing team. When they finally visited us in Nuernberg, they bored me with their glowing descriptions of their wonderful school, how much more they learned than we poor, small-town Bavarians, and how much they enjoyed the rowing competitions. We had difficulties in communicating for another reason, because they consciously talked in high German, Berlin-style, while we continued to speak our Bavarian dialect.

On the other hand, I bored them with my constant tales of my confirmation, and my newfound religion.

According to Jewish tradition, all the official rites and public prayers are the duty of the men. Women were not obliged to attend services, but, if they wished to come, they had to sit in the back or on the balcony behind a grill. The only duty of women was the lighting of the Sabbath candles and the observance of kashruth, the Jewish dietary laws.

The coming of age of a Jewish boy is celebrated on his 13th birthday, his Bar Mitzvah, when for the first time he reads from the Torah during the Sabbath service. This initiation into manhood is considered the most important event in a man's religious life, more important, for instance, than his wedding, and is followed by a lavish reception in his home, and the receiving of many valuable presents.

There was no ceremony to mark the coming of age of a Jewish girl until liberal congregations in the 19th century introduced a confirmation for girls, copied from the Protestant rite of confirmation. Nowadays, girls in liberal congregations have a Bath Mitzvah, imitating the Bar Mitzvah of the boys. (Bar Mitzvah means the duties of the son, and, accordingly, Bath Mitzvah are the duties of the daughter.)

We went to instruction in the fundamentals of our faith for three months before the great event. It was given by our Rabbi, Dr. Freudenthal, a wise and learned man. He inspired us, and I embraced the philosophy of Jewish liberalism with its simplicity of our faith in one God, and our duty to work for the coming of the messianic kingdom on earth. We Jews could not accept Jesus as our messiah, because our vision of the messianic time is the kingdom of God on earth, a world of peace, happiness, and social justice, while the life and death of Jesus was not followed by peace but by untold misery, brought about by warring factions of Christianity.

On the day before the confirmation, during the feast of Shabuoth, corresponding to the feast of Pentecost, we had an examination in the synagogue before our assembled relatives and friends. I was appointed to say the closing prayer, which ended with the Shemah Israel, the confession of our belief in one God. I said the prayer with deep conviction, and with the awareness that I could project my voice so that it filled the whole, huge building.

The confirmation itself, for which we wore white dresses like our Catholic schoolmates, consisted in the recital of prayers and poetry by various confirmants, and an address by Rabbi Freudenthal, and ended with his blessing, the same blessing spoken by the ancient high priests of the temple in Jerusalem.

I was still in a trance of emotion when we returned home, and all the relatives and friends came for the reception with their gifts, mostly books. Some of the books were so valuable that I carried them with me throughout my later wanderings. My most valued confirmation gift was a brand new bike. Not

long after the confirmation, summer vacation started in
Prussia.

While vacation in Bavaria was from mid-July to the beginning
of September, vacation in Prussia was from the middle of
June to August. The Ludwig girls came to Nuernberg while
we were still in school. After I was done with homework, I
went with Elvira, the only one who was homesick for Nuernberg, on rambling walks through the old city, visited the Ludwigshoehe, and went swimming. Then, as soon as our vacation started, the Ludwigs, my brother Heinz, Aunt Hede and I
left for Berlin. Elvira and I were intimate friends and I used to
call her my only sister.

We took the train that left Nuernberg at 11:00 a.m., a train
that I would take to Berlin many more times in my life. It was
always a great adventure, because we always went to the dining car for coffee and cake while the train, fortified by an extra engine, pulled slowly up the slope into the beautiful
mountains of Thuringia. The last hours of the train ride took
us through the reaches of the northern European low plains,
with waving wheat fields and little villages. This scenery did
not interest us any more, so we talked with our traveling
companions.

Aunt Toni was at the train station. We took our bikes out of
the baggage car and loaded them on top of a taxi that then
took us to her home in Friedenau. At home, a cold supper
awaited us on the balcony, as well as red currants with
whipped cream. I still cannot figure out how Toni managed
to accommodate three houseguests in the small apartment.
We used to call it the "Rubber Home" because it always
stretched out to hold us all. I remember that I slept in the
cramped room with my three cousins, and that we were
awakened each morning when the office help arrived to
work in the little, curtained-off cubicle that was the office.

During the few days before my cousins had to go back to school, we rode our bikes every day to the Grunewald and the Wannsee, and while our cousins went to school, Hede, Heinz and I explored Berlin by streetcar and bus. Hede also took us to museums and department stores, which were boring to us then, but which I appreciated in later years.

The most amazing thing in Berlin were the many relatives that I had never known before whom we visited, or who came to visit us. The reason that I had so many cousins, uncles and aunts in Berlin was that my grandfather's West Prussian relatives had left Tuchel and Thorn after World War I because it had become Polish, while they considered themselves German citizens. Their German patriotism was badly shaken when Hitler became the leader. Most of them emigrated to America, but a number of them perished in concentration camps.

Whenever Elfriede and Elvira were free, we went swimming together, and I was quite discouraged when they showed off their skills in gymnastics, which I could not begin to match. But, all in all, it was a wonderful trip, the last vacation of my childhood, because, after my return home, adolescence descended on me with the force of a sledgehammer. Shortly I would be interested in boys, much to the contempt of my cousins, who continued to be wholly absorbed in school and sports.

Linoleum cut done by Steffi in art class.

XX. Adolescence

I have mentioned before the great role that Tanzstunde played in the life of my mother and aunts. Now, the time was approaching when I would have my dance lessons in Mr. Krebs' establishment, and be introduced into society.

My own thoughts and ambitions were still far removed from flirting, the favorite activity of my schoolmates, because I was still a member of the Kameraden, the youth organization that shunned conventional society, especially ballroom dancing, alcohol, and smoking.

Finally, a young man named Karl Blumenthal, a serious fellow who wanted to be a rabbi, asked me to join him as his partner in the Tanzstunde. He fell violently in love with me, and I fell as violently in love with love.

Until then, I considered myself very unattractive. This was partly due to my mother's efforts to make me more attractive. She treated my freckles with bleaching cream, with the result that my face turned so pale that my freckles stood out worse than ever. She also made me wear rubber hosiery to give better shape to my fat legs.

Mama wrote in her diary at that time that she was worried about me because I was so unsatisfied and serious. No wonder--I was dissatisfied because of her constant nagging, which made me feel ugly. Her zeal to make me more attractive had one positive result. Unhappy about my slouching, she enrolled me in a special exercise class, which helped my coordination a lot.

As soon as I consented to participate in the Tanzstunde I got kicked out of the Kameraden. But, now, I was so deeply involved in my first love affair that I did not mind.

Karl went to the same school as my little brothers. They were our messengers and carried our frequent notes to each other.

Even now I blush when I think that the little boys eagerly read our silly declarations of eternal love. Karl and I remained inseparable friends throughout the year of the Tanzstunde and the parties that followed until we found out that the bond between us was infatuation, not love.

When I left the Kameraden, I joined another Jewish Youth organization, the "Judische Jugendbund." This was a middle-of-the-road club, sponsored by our other rabbi, Dr. Heilbrunner. Most of the participants of the "Tanzstunde" belonged to it.

During the school year of 1927-1928, my tenth year of school, I was so involved with Tanzstunde and Jugendbund that school receded into the background.

Yet, two of the most lasting experiences of this year were connected with school. A new student, Gerda, sat next to me, and we embarked on a deep friendship.

She repeated the tenth grade because she had trouble keeping up with her studies the previous year. Actually, she was the same age as we, but had entered school a year earlier than we, in order to be with her sister who was a year older. Gerda was a very unhappy girl. Her mother had died when she was young. Her father, a well-known gynecologist, had remarried a beautiful woman soon afterwards who was the bad step-mother as described in the fairy tales. Her stepmother stood between the children and their father, and their relationship with him was remote. Gerda had clung to her older sister, but now it was time that she had to stand up for herself.

I shared with her our admiration for our French teacher, Dr. Graf, as did many of our classmates. Dr. Graf was a liberal man who was not carried away by the Nazi propaganda. He showed his concern for us Jewish students. Many of us had a very personal relationship with him, and after the war was over, we who were now living in Israel or the U.S. got in touch with him. We corresponded with him, and whoever of his former students visited Germany made a pilgrimage to his little house in Lauf, a town that I knew so well, because it was near our beloved Ludwigshoehe.

Although he taught French, Dr. Graf's avocation was art. He would bring pictures of famous French artists like Rodin, Daumier, and the impressionists to class and explain them to us. As we got more and more interested in his art lectures, he shared with us pictures that had nothing to do with our French lessons. I especially remember the pictures of graphics artist, Kaethe Kollwitz, who portrayed the misery of women of the working class with deep understanding and compassion. By explaining her pictures to us, Dr. Graf gave us insight and social awareness, one of the most precious gifts that we got in our school years. I kept his lessons with me throughout my life.

Etching by Kaethe Kollwitz.

Actually, school was fun. When we went to the movies, all the students marched four abreast through the city streets to the theater. The most unforgettable movies we saw were Nanook, The Eskimo, Rin-Tin-Tin, and the Saga of the Nibelungs. On our hiking days we usually traveled by train into the lovely hills northwest of Nuernberg. As I was an experienced hiker, and could play marching music on the guitar, I was a valuable member of the class on such hikes. However, on regular school days, non-Jewish students rarely associated with us Jews. Dr. Graf went with his homeroom on these field trips, but he once devoted a Sunday to go on a

On the trip with classmates in a Youth Hostel (10th grade).

wonderful hike with my class. I will never forget the scrambled eggs that fell into the fire, which we ate with soot and dirt, and much glee.

It seems that Art with a capital A was the theme of this school year, because we also had a wonderful art teacher. She took the class out of the school building and let us sketch from nature either the quaint old buildings of our city or groups of trees. Fraulein Wuest also went with us on a memorable hike through the Franconian Swiss, the same tour that we had made years ago with our parents, and where we had returned many times since. We stayed overnight in a youth hostel, burnt our dinner, and sang and laughed deep into the night.

The art and culture game went even further. We seldom missed the monthly performances, presented especially for students, in the municipal opera house or the repertory theater, where we saw plays by the German classical poets as well as plays by Shakespeare, Bernard Shaw, and modern German authors. In addition, we went on our own to the many concerts that were offered in our city. Mama was still a member of the Chorus for Classical Music, and when she had a concert coming, my friend Maria Hirschmann and I went to at least one rehearsal as well as to the concert.

This seems to be a very full schedule, but there were also weekends that were as full as the schooldays. Saturday was, of course, the Tanzstunde. There were ten couples who had their lessons together, another group of 12 Jewish couples had their lessons on Sunday evenings, but all our parties were shared. I have described all the events of a Tanzstunde in my mother's story. Herr Krebs had not changed his routine, except that we learned the fox-trot, tango and slow waltz, while our mothers had danced fast waltzes, polkas and quadrilles. At our coming out party, we had no dancing cards, but promised our partners dances ahead. A popular girl had at least six to ten dances promised, and at the end we all got muddled up, and danced with whomever we found first.

The Opera House in Nuernberg.

After the lessons were crowned by the big ball, we continued the year with parties, given by members of the class. Sometimes, a number of parents rented a small ballroom together. We usually had a sit-down dinner and a dance afterwards, but the most important part of the festivities were the skits, musical numbers and toasts, performed and written by us.

The most original of all the parties was conceived and arranged by Mama's friend Lily, with her son Heinz, who together with me and two other girls hosted the party, with the whole family participating.

The invitations resembled a full-page ad for a grand sale of a well known department store which promised free refreshments, free samples of merchandise, fabulous entertainment provided by the guests, and dancing.

Our big house was ideally suited for this event. We had collected free samples of soap, perfume, toothpaste, skin cream, and stationery, which were arranged on sales tables in the two smaller rooms with roll upon roll of toilet paper as fillers.

Two of the other rooms were transformed into dining areas with small tables, a buffet of hot dogs and potato salad, a keg of beer, soft drinks, coffee, and numerous cakes. The hall was an ice cream parlor with an authentic ice cream stand, borrowed from the ice cream vendor across the street. The largest of the rooms was emptied for dancing. We had hired a pianist and a percussion battery, and most of the guests had prepared skits and songs for nonstop entertainment. The climax was a poem by Lily, that I recited while distributing little gifts with a personal meaning for each guest.

The costume party in our house.

The 10th grade ended with a formal graduation. For most of our classmates this was the end of their education, but others, especially the Jewish girls, went to business school, technical school, teachers' seminary, or art school.

Marianne Schmidt and I had missed the opportunity after the seventh year of school to transfer to the gymnasium where Latin was taught and where the students prepared for the abitur. But in the years when we graduated from high school, a three years' course that could be compared to junior college was instituted in our school. Girls from different schools were enrolled in this course, called Ober Realschule. The emphasis of our studies were math, science and modern languages with Latin as an optional subject.

Marianne and I were the only Jewish girls in our class.

Our Tanzstunde partners were mostly a year older than we. Most of them went to the gymnasium. Some of them had entered the business of their parents, or had positions in offices or stores. Some of them, like Heinz Bruckmann became traveling salesmen.

Many members of the Tanzstunde were also members of the "Jugenbund," and we continued to meet even after we were graduated from school. Our president was Georg Josephsthal, the son of a prominent family in Nuernberg. Georg was an exceptional young man: intelligent, idealistic, imaginative, energetic, fat, conceited, and a true, warm friend. At that time he was not yet a Zionist; he thought that a solution to the Jewish problem could be found here in Germany. We had many discussions about the "Jewish question," and ultimately he became an ardent Zionist who went on to become Golda Meir's foreign minister in Israel. Unfortunately for us, and for Israel, he died very young, in 1962. His future wife, Senta Punfut, was also a leader of our group.

Under Georg's leadership, the Jugendbund flowered into a great educational experience. We catered to all tastes. Besides weekly dances, we had seminars given by a young lawyer, about women's and children's rights, by an economist about economics, and by a social scientist about social problems. These were high-level courses, much more interesting than anything we learned in school. We had a dramatics group where we read plays and discussed books, and, of course, we went on trips.

It was my task to arrange for meetings and longer vacation trips with other groups of the Jugendbund in Bavaria, since I was a good organizer. We visited small Jewish communities in Bavaria, where we often found members of our families who still lived in small country towns. At that time I got interested in family research.

I usually carried my guitar with me wherever we went, and I had a great repertoire of serious and funny songs. I can see myself sitting in a meadow in a small village, singing, and collecting a small circle of listeners of local children when Joseph said admiringly, "I have never heard anybody sing so beautifully without having formal voice training.

During the summer of 1928, we made a memorable trip to Munich with my family. We spent much time there in the museums, and another few days at the Ammersee, where I broke a toe and where I got severe bronchitis. I was in bed with a high fever for a couple of weeks, the family doctor was on vacation and the substitute doctor said that my lungs were damaged and I should go for a cure to Berchtesgaden, to the inhalatorium in the salt mines. In the meantime, our family doctor returned, examined me, and said that nothing was wrong with my lungs, and it would be a pity to miss school for a month.

During the first fog in autumn, I suffered an attack of asthma, which would play such a terrible role in my life for the next forty years.

I was very depressed throughout the fall of 1928. It was not only the asthma, but I had broken up with my boy friend, Karl, and had fallen head over heels in love with his best friend, Arne Golden, a spectacular genius who looked like Apollo, and who already had two adoring girl friends to juggle around and could not accommodate a third one. Arne could sparkle like a firecracker, and then fall into a Mephistopheles-like brooding temper, which made him even more attractive to young females.

XXI. 1929

I suffered from asthma all through the winter and spring of 1929. Our family doctor suggested a long stay near the sea. Friends found a position for me as mother's helper in a children's home on the Island of Foehr in the North Sea. I stayed there for five weeks of my six-week summer vacation. It was a lonely time because the children were too young to be company, and the two sisters who owned and ran the home were too old to be companions. The weather was cool and rainy, so we could not swim. But rain or shine, I had to go to the beach every morning with the children, build sand castles, and play ball with them. Only twice was I able to go all by myself to another island on my two free Sundays. I was not paid, but got free food and lodging, and a minuscule amount of pocket money. On the other hand, I had all afternoons off, when I undertook long, solitary walks, listened to the band in the village square, ate a lot of candy, read numerous books, and wrote melancholy letters to my friends.

Only the last week of the vacation was truly happy. I took a ship from Foehr to Cuxhaven, passing near the famous island of Helgoland. It was a sunny day with a blue sea crowned by white tufts of surf, with seagulls following us all the way. The ship's name was "Eagle." I regretted that my parents had not allowed me to stop in Hamburg, a city of ill repute, but I dutifully took the train from Cuxhaven directly to Berlin.

I stayed in Berlin only a few days, but was happy to meet my Ludwig cousins again. On Sunday, we all went together to the airport, where we made our first flight in a small aircraft. The name of the airplane was "Sea Lion," and we laughed a lot about the fact that I made my first sea voyage with the "Eagle" the same week that I experienced my first flight on the "Sea Lion."

Yet, I was unhappy, and unfulfilled. With the first foggy day my asthma returned and life seemed to be meaningless. In short, I was loved by nobody, yearning to love and to be-loved. I thought that I was unattractive because I was slightly overweight and had freckles, and that none of our group of friends really liked me.

It was at Marianne Schmidt's birthday party that I fell deeply in love for the first time. I was quite innocent, although I had had several boy friends, had gone steady, and had had hopeless crushes. At age 17, I had never kissed a boy.

I was wearing a beautiful new dress of aquamarine silk that harmonized with my spectacular flaming red hair and, for once, I felt beautiful.

The big table was taken out of the dining room, and we sat at small card tables that would later be taken out to make room for dancing. Otto Bauer, my neighbor at the table, was an old acquaintance. He was the steady boyfriend of one of my girl friends, who was at a finishing school in Switzerland. Marianne had a crush on him, and though she did not really expect him to fall in love with her, she talked about nothing but him at school. I was already fed up with her ravings about him. But I had to admit that he was by far the most handsome boy in our group. With his athletic body, his shiny blond hair, his deep blue eyes and a bold nose in a perfectly chis-eled face, he looked more like an Aryan ideal of manhood than like a Jewish boy. Otto was also intelligent, charming, witty, was admired by his friends, and adored by his parents whose only child he was.

It never entered my mind that such a paragon might be in-terested in a nobody like myself.

At the dinner table, we had an animated conversation about the role of German Jews in society. Otto thought that the on-ly solution was a complete assimilation into German culture with conscious suppression of our so-called Jewish traits.

Otto.

I dared to contradict him. "The trouble with us Jews is that we are so competitive. We always want to be better than anybody else. We will never be able to enter the mainstream of German society as long as there are so few factory workers, craftsmen, and farmers among us."

"I don't understand you," said Georg Josephthal, the president of the Jugendbund. "You sound like an anti-Semite."

"You may be right," I replied. "Let me tell you what happened to me the other day."

I was amazed at how intently the three people at our table were listening to me as I told them my story.

"A girl in my class, Else Reichert, who is a professed Nazi, is sitting behind me. The other day she asked me for my math workbook to copy my homework, as many girls do all the time. I felt kind of honored that this fanatic Nazi girl asked for help from me, a Jew. She kept my notebook for quite a while, and when she finally returned it, it was plastered with hundreds of tiny swastikas. It was during class time, and I could only mutter 'What have you done?' She said, 'I'll talk to you later.' "

I stopped in my story, and saw three pairs of eyes looking at me, full of sympathy. Finally, Otto said, "Go on, what did she have to say?"

"Else was waiting for me in the hall as we filed out of the classroom. She said defiantly, 'You must agree with me that the Nazis are right--you Jews are a race of parasites within our nation. You people don't like to work with your hands and get dirty. Who has ever heard of a Jew doing an honest day's work on a farm or in a factory? All you know is making money and sucking the lifeblood out of hardworking people.' "

I looked around at my friends for their reaction, because my reaction to Else's words had been consternation, disbelief, and silence.

"Did you tell her that the Jews were forbidden to own land for many centuries, and could not become farmers?" asked Georg. His girl friend Senta explained, "None of the guilds admitted Jews, so Jews could not become craftsmen, except to supply the necessities of their own people."

Georg continued, "In the Middle Ages, when the roads were unsafe, nobody was willing to trade from place to place. Only the Jews had no choice but to risk their lives as traveling salesmen, because they had no other way to feed their families." Otto added, "Gentiles were forbidden by their religion to lend money for interest, so the despised Jews had to take over a necessary task in society, and became bankers."

"All of you are right," I said. "But I was unable to tell this to Else, because I was so flabbergasted. Anyway, she did not wait for an answer, but left me standing there speechless."

Since nobody commented, I continued, "The more I think about it, the more confused I am. I can see how her argument can convince people who do not know what you have just said. I did one thing. I went the same evening to a meeting of the Zionist organization and joined. I want to be part of a Jewish community in Palestine that would be self-sufficient, with Jews doing all the work that Else said the Jews are shunning. The young people in the Hechaluz, the pioneer organization, are now training to become farmers and craftsmen, and there are already Jewish farmers and craftsmen in Erez Israel, in Palestine. I think we can show the world and ourselves that Jews are no parasites, but can do every kind of work that is required."

"Do you think the Nazis are right?" asked Otto.

"Of course not, but I do not think that assimilation into the German society is a possible solution for us."

Georg said, "The Jugendbund is neither for assimilation nor for Zionism. All we do is study our history and culture. Knowing our heritage is the best defense to meet the onslaught of anti-Semitism. Of course, you still belong to us, even after you have joined the Zionists."

Otto danced with me that evening the first, the second, and the third dances, and then, footweary, we sat down together. I do not remember what we talked about, because I was lost in admiration as he towered above me while we danced.

When the evening was over, after he had walked me home, I felt as if I had drunk champagne all evening long. I was bubbling and dizzy, walking on clouds. His last words were, "See you tomorrow, at the hike."

Otto did not often go on the hikes of the Jugendbund. We hikers belonged to a different, less sophisticated crowd. Otto was an intellectual, and very refined, while we were a noisy, a bit vulgar bunch. Otto preferred to take part in our literary groups and seminars about social issues.

But, that Sunday Otto was already waiting with the hikers at our meeting place in front of the railway station. We took the train for half an hour to the foothills, and hiked briskly for about two hours. I had my guitar, and played marching songs, and all joined in singing.

When we stopped for lunch and rest at the edge of a meadow in the forest and sat down, I began to play a horrah, a Jewish folk dance that I had learned at the Zionist meeting. But nobody joined in because they did not know the Hebrew words. They listened politely, but I soon put my guitar down, and we ate our bag lunch.

After lunch the group started a ball game, as was our custom. Otto said to me, "I don't like to play ball. Will you keep me company?"

My heart missed a beat. Otto was asking me for my company! We strolled away from the noisy players until we found a perfect nest under the trees with the sun on our backs. We flung ourselves down on the grass and looked over the tree-framed meadow. Insects were buzzing above the grass, and an occasional bird twittered far away. The sky on this Indian summer day was a pale blue, and the shadows became longer and longer. I felt like an enchanted princess with her prince, as Otto reached over to hold my hand as we lay in the grass.

We never kissed or embraced each other this, nor any other, time. Yet, I felt nearer to him than I have ever felt with my other friends.

We talked about our families, and our life's ambitions. Otto told me about his materialistic father, so proud of his family, yet so uncouth, and only interested in earning enough money so that Otto and his sophisticated mother could live in the lavish style that she was accustomed to. To have such a beautiful and refined wife was his father's highest reward. When Otto talked about his beloved mother, his face lit up like the sun. She was an accomplished pianist who had relinquished a career as a concert pianist to marry and to live for her family; she understood literature and art, and had taught him to appreciate the refined pleasures of life. About himself, he said that he wanted to become a lawyer to work for justice, and to help the poor and suppressed.

I told him about my large, closely knit family, and about my cousin Fritz Ottensooser, a hematologist at the Ehrlich Institute in Frankfurt. He had inspired me to study science. I told him my innermost secret, that I wanted to study photosynthesis in order to duplicate the creation of sugar from water and oxygen in the air as the plants do, in the test tube, and eventually in industry. If I could succeed in this, there would be no more hunger in this world, no more wars.

I became excited and flushed as I put my ambition into words for the first time, an ambition that I would never achieve, and which has not yet been achieved.

I was in the middle of a sentence when a cool breeze announced the setting of the sun, soon followed by the shouts of our friends that it was time to go home.

Otto promised to call during the week to continue our conversation. The next weekend Otto went with me, Marianne and my family to the Ludwigshoehe to harvest the apples in our orchard. It was as happy an outing as the hike the week before, and Otto promised again to call me during the week.

He never called as I waited day in, day out near the telephone, thinking of nothing but my love for him.

Georg called me on Thursday of that week to tell me that Otto had an infection, had very high fever, and that his life was in danger. My world suddenly became a blank, I went through the motions of everyday life like a sleepwalker, and that night, I prayed.

Though I went regularly to the temple, and insisted that Jewish traditions were kept in our house, and though I believed in God, I seldom prayed.

My father had told me that prayer was selfish because we ask God only for our personal needs. God was far too great to listen to our petty requests, that we should not meddle with God's great plans that we mortals could never understand. He explained to me how in a war both parties pray for victory to the same God, and that innumerable crimes have been committed in the name of God and religion, that were supposed to be the ultimate good. Yet, this night, I was on my knees asking for Otto's life.

"If you are God, if you are good, what can the world gain from the death of this promising young man? God, I am not only asking for myself, but for mankind to whom he had vowed to devote his life, for his parents, for his friends who love him, and whose lives are enriched by knowing him."

Tears ran down my checks; I felt as if I was fighting with God for Otto's life. He appeared to me more and more as a young god as I continued to pray.

Otto had already joined God in heaven while I was praying and weeping. It was many years before I prayed again for a personal favor from God.

We had a memorial service on Sunday afternoon. The rabbi based his homily on the words of an old man who said, "Friend, in spring, I pick roses."

Later that year, we, Otto's friends, began to visit his mother, the beautiful person whom he adored so much. All of us became her friends and she became our advisor. Otto's parents found a new togetherness in their grief, and life went on without him.

———————●———————

Furniture made in Arthur's factory.

XXII. 1930

For a while after Otto's death, we were all deeply depressed, but by the time my 18th birthday came along, we celebrated with a big party in our house. On this occasion, my friends and I planned our winter vacation. None of us had enough money to go south to the Bavarian Alps, where there is always snow on Christmas. We decided to go north to the Thuringian Mountains. We made arrangements to stay at the schoolhouse in Sonneberg, waxed our skis, packed our knapsacks, and took the train on Christmas day, a day of sun and fresh, powdery snow.

The accommodations were atrocious. Our group of about 30 people slept in two schoolrooms on uncomfortable cots that were only suitable for little children. The toilets were all backed up. The whole building smelled of it, and the heat was too low.

We took it in stride during the first day, because skiing was wonderful. But later in the afternoon I had a bad fall and tore a ligament in my heel, so I did not mind that the snow melted. Instead of skiing, we hiked across the mountains, with me limping bravely along. On the third day, it rained. So we sat all day on the heated veranda of the "Inn of the Green Tree" and played paper and pencil games. We had to consume something at this restaurant because we had to use their toilet all day long.

Henceforth, whenever we had to go to a washroom, we went to the "Green Tree."

When it snowed again, I could not go with my friends to ski because of my sore heel. Heiner, one of the boys, stayed behind with me to keep me company. During New Year's night, we went for a walk together through the virgin snow under a moonlit, starry sky. We felt happy and warm, deep inside, but after the magic of that enchanted night faded away, we remained just good friends without the magic of love.

Several of our friends who had to work during the week joined us for New Year's holiday. They brought us the very disturbing news that our factory had burned down during the Christmas weekend. I called home, but my parents assured me that I need not worry because the loss was covered by insurance.

As soon as I returned home, I went to see the damage. The building was still standing; all the machines had been salvaged, the office was damaged by the water, but the upper floor, where the fire had started, ignited by a spark from the faulty chimney, was completely destroyed. On this floor, many rooms of finished furniture were stored. This furniture was already sold, and only waited for shipment.

The factory was soon repaired and worked full-force to reproduce the lost furniture. Nobody worried very much until it was time to ship the merchandise. During the six-month delay between order and delivery, Germany had suffered a bad recession, and our customers refused acceptance of the delayed delivery.

Papa was left with hundreds of pieces of furniture, and mountains of debts. He was facing bankruptcy.

I heard the bad news when I returned home after the most exciting summer of my youth. In order to describe this summer, I have to go back to the beginning of the year when I had trouble in school. I was never a good student in foreign languages, but this year our teacher was not only incompetent, he was a rabid Nazi who treated Marianne and me like outcasts. I lost all interest in studying French and English. I copied my homework from Marianne, who in turn copied my math homework, and cheated during the tests. Once I got caught and received an F in French, which bothered my parents more than it bothered me.

Mama's friend Lily had a glorious idea. "Why don't you send her to France to learn French?" she said. She had contemplated sending Heinz as an exchange student to France during the summer, but he was not interested, while I was absolutely delighted at the prospect.

Since the World War, France and Germany had remained enemies, but our foreign minister, Gustav Stresemann, and France's Premier, Aristide Briand, worked for better relations between the two nations, and a part of their efforts was a student exchange during the summer vacations that continued even after Stresemann's untimely death.

Since the summer vacation in Germany started earlier, the German students went to France first, and then returned to Germany with their French friends. All applications were sent to a central bureau and carefully matched. Before our vacation had started, I left on July 1, while my classmates were still in school, and took the train to Paris where my sister for the summer, Lydia Jouk, awaited me at the train station. Lydia's parents were Russian Jews, who spoke French with an accent, but Lydia was completely assimilated, and her friends were all non-Jews, which surprised me, because at home Jews associated with Jews, and non-Jews with non-Jews.

Lydia was brunette, petite and very attractive, with a retinue of devoted admirers. I arrived on a Saturday evening, and the following Sunday, Lydia had planned a picnic for me with her friends. We took a train to a nice resort on the bank of the Seine. It was quite different from my weekly hikes in Germany. We sat on the bank all day long, swam from time to time, and danced to the music of a portable record player. Lydia and her friends smoked and drank a lot of wine, which was taboo on our outings. I could neither understand their conversation, nor did I dare to speak, so I remained an outside observer all day long.

For the next two weeks, Lydia had to go to school, and after school she had to study for her final examination.

I did not mind, because I was not lonely during those two weeks. Papa had business friends in Paris. One of them was an older, married man who invited me for a typical French gourmet dinner, and afterwards took me to the Tusseaud Wax Museum and the Eiffel Tower. He had no children of his own, treated me like a daughter, and was patient with my halting French.

More exciting was a young couple, exceptionally attractive people who went with me to a "Boite," a small nightclub with excellent performers of French songs in the style of Edith Piaf. Mrs. Zadek was a designer, and she made sketches of the artists, which she gave me after they were autographed. She also designed a party dress for me, which I later had made in Germany. An old bachelor cousin, Hermann Ottensooser, who was quite rich, lived in Paris. He was happy to meet me in the Cafe de la Paix, across from the opera, and after he had treated me to ice cream, coffee and cake, showed me around, and took me to the Louvre, or other museums. I also went to the Louvre and the nearby department stores on my own. But thing really got moving when Lydia finished school and we met most afternoons with her group of admirers in a cafe in Mont Parnass, or on the Boulevard St. Michel. We went together to the movies, to the theater, to museums, to Versailles. By that time I was able to converse in French, and they were proud to show me their incomparable city, while talking about philosophy and poetry.

This generation of French students loved to read the poems of Paul Verlaine, beautiful, decadent, and melancholic verses. Lydia gave me a book of his poems, and read many of them to me. The group was impressed when I told them that I had been with the Zadeks in the "Boite" where Verlaine drank himself to an early death. I showed them the sketches with the autographs of the artists. It seems that high school students were not allowed to go to nightclubs. They were grateful when I distributed some of the sketches among them.

When the German exchange students returned home with their French "brothers" and "sisters," all of us who were in Paris, a group of more than a thousand young people, were invited for a reception in the Palace of the French Foreign Minister in the Quai d'Orsay. After a nice speech, we had a garden party and were treated to ice cream, lemonade and petit fours. I stayed in Paris for another week after the party, and, at last, the Jouk family car that was in the repair shop all through the summer was repaired. For a glorious finale we had a family outing in Fontainbleau, a castle in the hunting forest of past French kings.

Lydia and I did not go directly to Nuernberg, but joined my friends from the Jugendbund on a tour of the Black Forest.

We took the train to Freiburg, where we were guests of my father's cousins, the Brauns of Freiburg, who lived in the middle of the old university town, across from the cathedral. After two days, my friends arrived in Freiburg, and we continued together on a hiking trip through the Black Forest.

The first day of our trip was extremely strenuous. We hiked over 20 miles that day, swam in the Titisee, and climbed the Feldberg, the highest mountain in the Black Forest. We were quite exhausted and had many blisters on our feet when we reached the Spartan youth hostel, where we would spend the night. Lydia was not accustomed to hiking for long distances, nor was she accustomed to the rigors and simplicity of a youth hostel. She was raving mad at me for having exposed her to such hardship. I was footsore myself, and not in a mood to put up with her abuse. We had a memorable fight, but there was no way to send Lydia home. She was ready to take the next train back to Paris, but we were far from any train station. She had to limp along on sore feet in her unpractical high heeled shoes, until a rainy day stopped us, and we remained in a lovely inn in the middle of the Black Forest, recovering from our exertions. Lydia mellowed under the loving care of my friends, and became a good sport after her blisters had healed. We took the train to Lake Constance (Bodensee), went sightseeing in Constanz, and took a boat ride on the lake. Instead of hiking, we swam and rowed on the lake, and Lydia eventually got reconciled to sleeping in a dormitory in the youth hostel.

Lydia's stay in Nuernberg was much less successful than my visit to Paris. When I had to go back to school, Lydia spent most of the time with another French exchange student, much younger than she, and they spoke French instead of learning German. However, we spoke German together when we went swimming with my friends. It was still warm enough to go swimming. Most of us were members of the swimming club Blau-Weiss, which owned a tiny lake surrounded by a large meadow half an hour by bike from our house. There we spent most of our afternoons after school swimming and playing ball games with my friends, and doing our homework, helping each other. Later, all Jewish members were asked to resign, but while Lydia was in Nuernberg we were still accepted.

Lydia and I parted as good friends and corresponded for a few years, at longer and longer intervals until we finally lost touch with each other.

While I was in France with Lydia, my father faced bankruptcy. However, his relatives, the Ottensoosers, his bankers, came to his rescue, and he was able to settle with his creditors. The Braun relatives, owners of the family furniture retail store, had an agreement with my father that gave them a monopoly as the sole retailers of his furniture in our area. They agreed that he could sell directly from the factory, in one big sale, all the furniture that had been refused after it was six months late. This sale was a resounding success, because we could undersell all competition by omitting the middleman. Papa decided to produce furniture to sell directly from the factory to the consumers. This was a breach of his agreement with his brother and nephews and resulted in a bitter family feud.

For me, the sales exhibition was a great challenge, because my father trusted my taste, and let me choose accessories, such as table settings, vases, pictures, bedspreads, vanity bottles and cosmetics, books for the bookcases. These articles were lent to us by the stores in return for the publicity. I spent happy hours arranging the furniture into comfortable, livable rooms that would appeal to customers.

In spite of the great success of the sale, household expenses had to be cut and we had to leave our grand villa in Kobergerstrasse for a modest apartment in the Sandstrasse. Our maid had to go, and poor Maria was saddled with housecleaning as well as cooking, and finally, even Mama had to get her hands dirty, helping her.

Now we lived a long way from school, but Martin Wollner, a friend from the Jugendbund, lived just around the corner, and for the next few months of school we walked to school together. We became very dear friends, and even thought we were in love.

———————●———————

Floh and I on our hitchhiking tour.

Last look to the Alps. The van in which we hitchhiked from Garmisch to Munich.

XXIII. 1931

The Sandstrasse was a drab street with large five-story soot-blackened sandstone apartment houses without any front gardens. Our dark apartment was on the first floor. When we opened the windows, the dust and noise of the busy thoroughfare were overpowering. The only redeeming feature was a small, glass-enclosed veranda off our parents' bedroom, that opened into a cemented, plantless back yard.

My three brothers shared a bedroom that contained three beds, many wardrobes, and nothing else. We called it "The Army Barracks."

The most beautiful room, with an elaborate, glazed-tile stove, was furnished with my own green furniture. I slept on a green couch, and a deep green carpet and green velvet drapes were added. It was now our salon, very distinctive and beautiful, but no longer my own.

The family room, where we had to eat in bad weather, was in a corner of the apartment and was only accessible through my room or our parents' bedroom because it had no outlet to the hall. Maria also had lost her privacy because the linen closet was in her tiny room.

The bathroom was a dark and narrow affair with the door on one end and a window at the other. It contained the washbasin, a hamper, the bathtub, the gas water heater and a gas space heater. Fortunately, the commode was in another little cell. Otherwise we, a family of seven, could not have managed. Even so, it was hard because Papa and we children needed the washroom at the same time in the morning. Papa would stand in front of the mirror above the washbasin and shave while the four of us scrambled around the bathtub faucet to perform our skimpy ablutions and brush our teeth. This was the only time of the day that I met my father during the week, because he usually came home very late in the evening when I was already out of the house with my social activities. Papa usually lectured us during the time he shaved, told us about the business, asked about our schoolwork, and scolded us if our grades were not topnotch.

As Christmas approached, we planned for the winter vacation. This year we decided to go south to the Bavarian Alps where we could always find good skiing conditions. The price of the trip was quite high, and no money was left for a skiing outfit. I had the skis and boots, but no suit. I suggested waterproofing my sweatsuit, which was not very fancy, but was warm enough. Mama agreed, and I went to buy a waterproofing chemical that had to be dissolved in gasoline. After I came home with the can of gasoline, Mama and I went to work. I turned off the great switch that brought gas to the pilot of the water heater, and was confident that I had shut off all the gas in the bathroom. We soaked the garments in the solution, and then started to wring the liquid out, each of us holding one end of the suit, when the big bang occurred, and the room was full of fire. I let go of the suit, and ran out into the hall shouting, "Help, Fire!" at the top of my lungs. I was screaming like mad, running senselessly toward the street, when Maria came out of her room, yanked me back and rolled me on the floor, until the fire in my clothes was extinguished. When she was done with me, she looked for Mama who stood, still completely dazed, in the bathroom with the burning rag in her hands. She put Mama in bed, called the fire station, and tried to call a doctor.

Maria was still on the phone trying to locate a doctor when the firemen came. There was nothing left for them to do. The fire had burned itself out. Only a rag that had once been my sweatsuit was still smoldering on the tile floor. Not much damage was done to the room or the house. Windows shattered up to the fifth floor, a crack in the corner over the space heater, and soot covering the walls were the only signs of the explosion. But Mama was crying out in terrible pain. Her face was so swollen she could not open her eyes, and her face and hands were covered with huge blisters and black, third-degree burns. Each of her screams pierced my heart with guilt. I was aware that I was the culprit because I forgot to check the pilot light on the space heater that was still burning after I thought I had shut off the gas.

Our family doctor was on vacation and so was his replacement. Finally, Maria found Dr. Stephan Wurzinger, Aunt Ada's former boyfriend, a pediatrician.

He bandaged mama's hands and gave her a shot of morphine, before Maria and I undressed her and put her in a clean bed. Days of agony followed for Mama. All her wounds got infected and it took several days until we were sure that her eyes were alright. Stephan was not trained in treating burns, and did everything wrong, but Mama refused to call another doctor because she liked Stephan. It took several months for the burns to heal, leaving ugly, permanent scars.

Maria was heroic in her care of Mama. She washed her, fed her, and put her on the potty, while cooking and cleaning the house at the same time. I did all the shopping, some of the cooking, and took care of the constant flow of visitors, feeling guilty beyond description.

Adding to Mama's physical sufferings came the pain about Papa's neglect of her. While she was busy arranging our new apartment and lifestyle, she was only dimly aware how late Papa came home, later than ever before. He told her that the business demanded his attention, and she sadly agreed. Now, in her terrible suffering when she needed Papa's support more than ever, he completely let her down, and she cried herself to sleep, long before he came home. Finally, the bubble burst. Mama found out that Papa had had a girlfriend for a couple of years and she was outraged. But the reason for her deep shock was not that Arthur had been unfaithful to her -- that was old hat -- but the fact that he had concealed his affair from her. Both my parents valued honesty over and above all other virtues, and from the outset of their married life had promised never to have secrets from each other and to discuss each problem freely with their partner. When Papa was unfaithful in the past he confessed to her, even asked her to concede that it was his godgiven right to release his tensions when he felt it necessary. Mama was dejected and unhappy for a few days, cried until her eyes were red and inflamed, and then, after a rewarding reconciliation, forgave him and loved him more than ever because of his strong masculinity.

This time it was different. She could not forgive him his dishonesty, his deceit. She considered divorce as well as suicide, but was much too sick for either. Maria was her greatest support during this crisis, because she could not speak with any other person about her problem.

Her good friends, Lily and Erna Braunger, were of no great help during Mama's ordeal because they had problems of their own.

Erna, the piano teacher, had developed arthritis in her hands and could no longer play or teach. In addition to this misfortune, her friend had a reconciliation with his wife and broke up his relationship with her. Erna never became a Nazi. She continued her friendship with Mama until my parents left Germany, but it was a frustrated and sad Erna who died a lonely death a few years after the war ended. She and Mama corresponded until her death.

An even worse fate was in store for Lily. At the time of Mama's accident, she became more and more morose and withdrawn, until she lost contact with reality. I once visited her with Mama. I barely recognized the unkempt, raving woman with wisps of white hair hanging into her heavily mustached face. She recognized neither Mama nor me. Soon afterwards, her husband Oskar had to send her to an asylum.

While she was there, Mama faithfully visited her once a month. Each time she returned in deep despair, because Lily had not recognized her, and was living in an imaginary hell of prosecution and fear.

Finally, just before Hitler decided to terminate all the inmates of insane asylums, she got well enough to go home and join Oskar and her son Heinz. But Heinz contracted tuberculosis and had to be sent to a sanatorium in Switzerland, where he later died as a young man.

Mama visited her often but Lily was only a shadow of her former witty self. When my parents left Germany in 1939, Lily and Oskar remained in Germany. They were deported to Theresienstadt, from where they never returned.

Floh had known for some time that Papa was having an affair with one of his employees, and was chasing young apprentice girls through the long hall of his furniture exhibition, because Floh was working as a carpenter's apprentice in the factory. He finally told me all that he knew about our father's escapades, and I was absolutely shocked. Floh was also deeply disturbed.

We finally reproached Papa one morning while he shaved and we brushed our teeth. Papa was completely defensive and said that men need more than one woman to fulfill their sexual needs, while women are quite content to be faithful to their spouse. Mama did not attract him any more sexually, while he treasured her highly as a companion and a person. He did not want a divorce at all, but he wanted her and us children to understand his needs and to consent to his finding sexual release elsewhere.

I was torn apart. I could not condone what Papa was doing. I loved Mama deeply, and resented that he made her so unhappy. But this man was my father, whom I loved dearly.

What could I do? Besides everything, this open discussion of "forbidden" subjects aroused my own, yet unfulfilled, sexual drives.

For a long time Mama was so absorbed in her despair that she lost interest in her family and neglected us, we who were accustomed to her warm love and interest in our lives. Three of us, Werner, Floh and I were able to give Mama our love and understanding. Only Heinz went to pieces.

He felt unloved, unwanted, and incompetent. His grades in school went down and he was gloomy and unresponsive. While all the rest of the family blamed him for being stubborn and uncooperative, I made it my own project to get through to him and made a conscious effort to spend as much time as I could, playing games with him or taking him to the movies. Sometimes I believed that I had gotten through to him while at other times I felt that I had failed him, but later that year, inadvertently, I was able to help him to find self-confidence and success.

Before I can write about this momentous event, I have to write about my own experiences during spring and summer of 1931.

It seems that we were all so absorbed in our own personal problems that we did not notice the rising wave of anti-Semitism sweeping across Germany. Actually, it was our non-Jewish friends and acquaintances who made it a point to show us their resistance to the growing tide of Hitler's party.

The sphere of interest in the Jugendbund changed slowly. When Georg Josephthal was our president, we studied cultural and social problems that were connected with the depression in Germany. After Georg left Nuernberg to study jurisprudence in Munich, Martin Wollner became our president and began courses in Jewish history, Zionism and Hebrew.

Martin was my steady companion during 1931 but I could not fully return his warm friendship because of my infatuation for Arne. He was studying medicine at Erlangen, the small university within commuting distance from Nuernberg. He lived at home and often visited me on his way from the train station to his house, basking in my unwavering admiration without returning my love and warmth. However, he gave me a wonderful gift. We both loved music and went to the same concerts and operas. Before each performance he came to our house and explained the music to me and played some of the themes on the piano so that I was able to follow and understand the music.

During those months, I worked hard in school to prepare for the abitur, the final examination after 13 years of school, which was the entrance exam for the university. Since Papa's financial difficulties, I had given up hoping to be able to study chemistry but was resigned to work in the factory after school was over. It was no easy decision, and did not dampen my ambition to pass the abitur with high grades.

The abitur was a grueling, complex, comprehensive examination that lasted for two weeks, including written tests of four hours each in German, English, French, math, physics, chemistry, Latin, and art, and oral examinations in some of the same subjects. I did very well on my tests and everybody in the class passed easily. After the ordeal of the test, we classmates celebrated together and lo and behold, even Marianne and I were included in the festivities.

Before I even knew my grades, I got a call from our rabbi, Dr. Freudenthal, who said that he would like to see me. I went to his office at the synagogue where he received me with a big smile.

"Congratulations, Steffi. You got the best grades in your class in the abitur. What are your plans?"

I told him at length about my intention to study chemistry and my reasons for it, and about my disappointment that my parents would not be able to afford my studies. He said that the Jewish congregation had a scholarship fund to pay tuition for young students who showed promise, and he would use his influence to award me a scholarship.

After a few days of suspense he called me back to inform me that I was a recipient of a scholarship, covering all my tuition expense.

I was thrilled, as were my parents, who decided that I would study in Erlangen and continue to live at home. However, I had to change my plans and take a curriculum that would prepare me for a more practical career as a science teacher. When I finally enrolled at the university, I took chemistry as my major with physics and biology as my minor subjects, after I had discussed my plans with Dr. Freudenthal.

Just after graduation, I got a visit from my former school friend, Ilse Jaeger, who had moved with her parents to Hoehr, a small town near Koblenz, where her parents had a business in ceramic materials and where she went to a school that taught pottery-making.

Ilse and I had a few wonderful days, visited our childhood paradise on the Ludwigshoehe, and met with former school friends. Then her older brother Rolf came to pick her up with his little two-seater Hanomag to return home. Ilse and Rolf suggested that I accompany them, riding on the rumble seat. Ilse and I took turns on that hard and uncomfortable seat.

The trip to Koblenz took us through lovely mountains and old towns, and once, near Frankfurt, we passed a small airport which specialized in flying lessons in a small two-seater open airplane. Rolf dared us to fly in that flimsy contraption. Of course, we took his challenge and he paid for a 20 minute flight for each of us. I was the first, and got strapped on top of a parachute with a flight-stick between my legs on the back seat of the tiny plane. The instructor flew low over treetops and villages; the stick between my legs moved as he steered the plane. The wingtips seemed to be vertical whenever he made a turn. I trembled with fright and delight. After Ilse had her turn, we went to the next village and drank wine to steady ourselves again after the exciting experience.

Ilse's parents were delighted to see me again, and were perfect hosts. The atmosphere in the Jaeger family was peaceful and serene. Ilse's father, with his gentle humor, was so different from my overpowering father that it was nerve-soothing to be with them after that winter in our turbulent household.

We went to the old town of Koblenz for sightseeing and shopping. We took a pleasant ride in a boat on the Rhine river, with vineyard-covered hills on both sides, and castles and ruins of old castles on top of the hills. Ilse's mother was with us, and invited us for coffee and cake in one of the castles that was restored and converted into a restaurant. Ilse and I went for many walks in the hills, talking about ourselves, our plans, our ideals, our boyfriends, and felt very close to each other. Ilse was so much more steady than I. I had the impression that she was much older and wiser and I loved her deeply.

After a week, Rolf had to drive again to Nuernberg, and I rode with him in the front seat. We drank wine on the way and got high and animated. We had a wonderful time and when we arrived home, late at night, we parted with a warm, friendly kiss.

I enjoyed a month of vacation before I started at the university. I found a student to tutor, helped in the business, and met my old friends who were home from their universities for the spring vacation.

School started in May. Erlangen is a small town, a county seat. The count of Erlangen had founded a Lutheran theological school about a hundred years ago that had grown into a full university over the years. The former residence of the count was now the administration building. Behind the palace was a beautiful park, imitating on a small scale the gardens of Versailles, and around the park were the buildings of the different departments of the university. When we went from class to class, we had to cross and recross the park. All lectures began a quarter past the hour, and lasted 45 minutes, which was enough time to get from place to place, though many students used bikes. I often rode my bike on Mondays to Erlangen and left it there until I rode home on it Friday. The train ride took 30 to 40 minutes, but the bike route was shorter. It took an hour and a half to go from Nuernberg to Erlangen.

Lectures were a little turbulent because the students showed approval by scraping noisily on the floor and their disapproval with vehement stomping. Many students belonged to fraternities and lived in fraternity houses. They were easily spotted because they wore military hats and sashes with the colors of their fraternity. Their favorite activities were drinking beer in nightlong beer sessions, and fencing. Dueling with swords was forbidden by law in the republic, but had been legal during the time of the empire. Many doctors and lawyers proudly displayed the scars they received during their years as students, and wore them like badges of honor, proving their courage. Though duels were illegal now, every so often a student would show up with a heavily bandaged head, reeking of antiseptics. The fraternities, called Burschenschaften, had started around 1848, when the student revolts helped to bring about a united Germany. Now most fraternity members were fanatical patriots, and belonged to the rightist parties. Most finally joined the Nazi movement, except for one Catholic fraternity whose members wore the colors of the pope, white and yellow.

Nobody checked on student attendance. It was enough to pay tuition and know the subject matter at the final comprehensive exam. No credits or grades were given. However, for lab courses, the signature of the professor was needed to show that one had done all the prescribed experiments. Each department gave scholarship tests at the end of each semester for the recipients of scholarships. The professor who administered these tests in the chemistry lab was an old, senile fellow who had all his work done by his assistant, Leonhard Birkhofer. I met Leonhard first when I had to take my test. Later we became good friends.

I had a busy schedule, with three lectures scattered around the campus and two time-absorbing lab courses in chemistry and zoology. Our zoology professor, Dr. Fleischmann, was very old and did not believe in evolution. He spent most of the time in lectures trying to disprove the theory of evolution. He also used the lab course in embryology to show that the embryo does not go through the steps of evolution. What we did in the lab was to prepare microscope slides that we were allowed to keep for our future careers as teachers. Of course, we also dissected many animals and insects. I had to do my work over and over again and spent many extra hours in the zoological lab because I was so clumsy.

Nevertheless, I found time to go swimming on many afternoons with newly found boyfriends whom I juggled around the way I had learned from Arne with his girlfriends.

Arne played the same game with Annamarie that he had played with me, encouraging my crush on him while he himself was in love with two other girls. She was deeply and hopelessly in love with him, while he just strung her along with the rest of his harem. Annamarie was pathetically unhappy and I did my best to comfort her. I felt old and wise, since I had gone through the same experience.

I spent the weekends at home. On Friday nights after the Sabbath services, Dr. Freudenthal used to invite young people to his house for dinner and entertainment. Since my longer conversations with him about my plans and outlook on life, I had become one of his protegees, and was often invited. Mrs. Freudenthal was a perfect hostess. Food and wine were always excellent, but were overshadowed by the great pleasure of being with such brilliant young people. Many of Dr. Freudenthal's protegees were budding musicians, as was his own son, and we always had musical entertainment followed by spirited discussions. I had begun to write by that time, and sometimes read some of my poems. I was very proud to belong to this group of the cream of the crop.

The semester ended in July. Through Dr. Freudenthal's help, I got an interesting job during the month of August in Anna Esslinger's Waldschulheim, a famous boarding school in Herrlingen near Ulm on the Danube River.

It was a progressive school which experimented with new programs and that, along with another school in the same town headed by Anna's sister, made Herrlingen a household word in modern education. During summer the teachers were on vacation but the school could not close because some of the children had no place else to go. In addition, about 10 children came to spend the summer at the school. I was housemother in charge of about 20 children between eight and twelve years of age. The house was comfortable and roomy. The furniture of one of the schoolrooms was taken out to make room for a ping-pong table; another classroom was used as a study. The food was nutritionally balanced and very tasty. we all looked forward to each meal. The home, which was away from the village at the edge of the forest, had a large garden. One house, used during the school year as a dormitory, was closed during the summer. However, in both schools several children came down with measles and the house was used as a quarantine center for them.

I usually played ball games with the children in the mornings, and took them swimming or for long walks in the forest in the afternoons. When the weather was bad, I organized paper and pencil games and endless ping-pong tournaments.

My salary was very small but to make up for it Anna encouraged me to invite friends and family to spend a few days with us. I had one free afternoon a week which I used to spend in the nearby city of Ulm, where two former school friends of my mother were living. One of them had a son my age. We became good friends and went rowing together in the lagoon in the city park, and afterwards went to movies.

One day my little brothers came to Herrlingen on a hiking tour with the Kameraden. After their friends left for home, Heinz and Werner stayed for another week with me in Herrlingen. When it was time for them to return home, they begged me to let them hitchhike to the home of the Zeppelin on the Bodensee (Lake Constance), and take the train home from there. The Zeppelin was a well-known navigable balloon. I agreed, filled their knapsack with sandwiches and fruit and bade them godspeed. I had forgotten all about them until I got a frantic telephone call from home a few days later. Mama asked me what had happened to the boys, who had not yet arrived home. She was very mad at me when I told her that I had given them permission to see the Zeppelin. More than a week of desperate waiting followed until Mama called again to say that Heinz and Werner had arrived home, dirty and smelly, with their pockets full of onions and extremely happy.

They had hitchhiked from Friedrichshafen into the Bavarian Alps, slept in barns and once in a shelter for the homeless, and made it a sport to spend as little money as possible. When they heard that the pastor in a certain village fed vagabonds and hobos every evening, they went to him to eat with them. Several times they were picked up by the police as runaways.

Every time they were stopped, the policeman took a little notebook out of his pocket to check the names of all the children reported as missing. Our boys had a membership card for youth hostels and enough money to show, and they were not yet reported as missing. So, whenever they were picked up, Heinz boldly said, "We are no runaways; we are not in your book. We are hiking with the permission of our family." Heinz was fourteen and the protector of his thirteen-year-old brother, Werner. Once they got a ride from a homosexual who treated them to a nice meal in a posh restaurant. But when he got aggressive after the meal, the boys managed to run away. Finally, they decided that it was time to head homewards. Their last ride was in a truck full of onions where they sat in the open air, shivering with cold, and eating onions.

Heinz had grown up during that week. He conquered his feelings of inferiority and was a happy, confident youngster for the rest of his childhood.

Floh listened with great interest to all the tales. Actually, I heard the whole story from him, and he suggested that the two of us should make a similar trip when my time in Herrlingen was over. I was delighted with the idea, and Floh came to Herrlingen. We spent a day in Ulm, which is an old, medieval town with one of the most beautiful cathedrals in Germany and then took the train to Friedrichshafen. Unfortunately, we did not see the Zeppelin, which had taken off for South America the day before our arrival. We hitchhiked to Lindau, a picturesque little old town on an island in the Bodensee. We slept in the youth hostel, but later we followed the example of our little brothers and slept in barns.

It was a great experience to sleep in a barn in the fragrant hay, and usually the farmer invited us to eat with his family. One rainy night we knocked late on the door of a farmhouse. The friendly farmer said we could not sleep in the barn -- I don't remember why -- but he invited us to sleep on the hard, leather-covered sofas in the living room. We shared a simple supper of boiled potatoes and sour cream with the family and went to sleep. I slept soundly into the morning, but Floh was awake when the old farmer came in the room, stood before me and murmured "What a beautiful, girl," while looking at me. Floh and I got many rides but hiked in between the scenic attractions and swam in cold mountain lakes. I introduced Floh to his first cigarette which he smoked reluctantly, with much coughing. We tramped from Germany into Austria, and back to Germany.

One day we came to the highest mountain of Germany, the Zugspitze, which is shared by Austria and Germany. We would have liked to take the aerial tramway to the top but decided that it was too expensive. Instead, we climbed over a lower pass from Austria into Germany, picking and eating berries all the way.

It was not until 1979, 48 years later, that I was able to go up to the Zugspitze, with my husband.

From the Zugspitze, Floh and I came to Garmisch Partenkirchen, where we slept in the youth hostel and visited the spectacular Partnachklam, a very narrow canyon between steep rocks. Our last hitchhike was in an empty furniture van. Floh and I sat in absolute darkness on old blankets. Suddenly the van stopped. The driver and his companion opened the door for us and said, "Get out and have a last look at the Alps before we get to Munich." They took pictures of us, the van, and the mountains, which they later sent to us. They also shared some of their refreshments.

In Munich, where we slept in the youth hostel, we spent our final vacation days in the museums, especially in the German Museum of Science and Industry. This museum was the first of its kind, with life-size replicas of mines and factories, collections of automobiles and railway cars, and models of tunnels and bridges in various stages of construction. There were chemistry and physics experiments that the visitors could activate. It took days to see all of the museum, which was later imitated by the Museum of Science and Industry in Chicago. At The Munich Museum, our feet got more tired than on any of our long hikes, and we enjoyed every minute of it.

The second semester started in October. I worked in the family business for the rest of the summer and fall. The factory was on a side street near the city park and hard to find. Therefore, Papa had rented a small store in Fuerth where the streetcars from Nuernberg stopped.

It had no show window, but we were separated from the street view by a full length curtain. I did some bookkeeping, read or studied, or had visits from my friends while waiting for customers to take to the factory. One evening, Martin came to keep me company. That night we were open late, and I turned on the light while we sat together and kissed and necked. Suddenly, another friend burst in on us and cried, "Do you know what you are doing?" A crowd had assembled before the store, watching our activities which were silhouetted, like in a shadowbox, on the screen of the curtain. I had never felt so embarrassed in my life.

Mama had to take my place in the little store when I returned to the university. My next semester was less satisfying than the first because I felt the growing anti-Semitism among the student body, especially in the botanical lab course where I was avoided and was the only Jewish student.

Every year the students and staff of the chemistry lab had a Christmas party which was famous for its spirited fun. Everyone in the lab was going except Robert, the only other Jewish student, and me, because nobody asked us. Robert did not care but I was irked, because it showed how isolated both of us were from the rest of the students. Eventually, Leonhard Birkhofer, one of the lab assistants, asked me to be his date. The party was enjoyable and the beginning of a rewarding friendship.

XXIV. 1932, Berlin

I had a very unsettling experience in winter 1932. In Germany and other predominantly Catholic countries, the prelenten season is celebrated as "Fasching" or Mardi Gras. It is a time of wild parties, costume balls, sessions of ribaldry, a time of extravagance and sexual excess.

At 20 years of age, I was still considered too young to participate in the grand gala occasions in theaters or public dance halls, but I was invited to many private parties which, unbeknownst to my parents, sometimes got quite out of hand.

I was at one of those parties where a room had been emptied of furniture and was supplied with pillows and mattresses. The lights were dimmed and the couples enjoyed themselves, necking and kissing.

At that party, Arnold, a married man, father of two little children, fell violently in love with me. It was really not love, but infatuation and desire. I did not want to get involved with a married man, but was quite high on booze as well as flattered that a grown-up man, a pillar of society, admired me. I had the good sense not to go too far, and when the party was over the whole episode was finished for me. However, he called to say that he wanted to see me again. I refused, as was expected from a good girl like me.

Several days later his wife called me. I was embarrassed, but had a clear conscience. To my amazement, she did not call to make reproaches. On the contrary, she asked me to meet her husband again because he was so despondent that he had threatened to kill himself if he could not have me. She begged me to see him. She even said she would rather agree to a divorce than to see him so depressed. Of course, I melted. When I finally met Arnold, he asked me to go on a trip with him. I said no, but I said also that I liked him and was flattered by his love for me. I met Arnold several times during the next weeks. He became more and more ardent and infatuated. I, myself, was completely mixed up, not knowing how to handle my problem.

Of course, I could have gone to bed with him, but earlier my father had extracted a promise from me, that I remain a virgin until I was married, or at least 25 years old, and I felt obliged to honor my word.

Finally, two of Arnold's friends intervened. They were a warm, understanding couple. They invited me, along with Arnold and his wife, to dinner. I don't remember the conversation; it was extremely emotional and, when I returned home, in my excitement I told my parents about my dilemma. They were understanding and helpful, maybe proud that I confided in them, and suggested sending me to Berlin to stay with Aunt Toni, to break up this unhealthy relationship. They even suggested that I might continue my studies in Berlin while living with her family.

It was only two weeks before the end of the semester. I was able to get full credit for my lab courses, and to hell with the lectures. On my last day in Erlangen, I took my suitcase along, and took the train from Erlangen to Berlin.

Since my last visit to Berlin, Toni and Hans had bought a large, old villa with a garden, big rooms, and ample space in the basement for the office and warehouse. Toni was glad to welcome me, though they had no room for me because part of the house was sublet, and I had to camp on the living room sofa, which created problems because the Ludwigs liked to stay up late and get up late, while I liked to go to bed before midnight, and get up early. I often fell asleep while they were still sitting around the table.

The Ludwig's maid had left shortly before my arrival, and Toni was looking desperately for a replacement. In the meantime, the family rarely had a warm meal because Toni was working in the business and the three girls were working or going to school. My cooking skills were practically nil, but, with great effort and good will, I managed from time to time to put an edible, hot meal on the table.

As soon as I arrived, I tried to register at the university, but was told that they already had more students than they could handle. It was the same story at the Institute of Technology. My cousin Elvira was taking courses in at the Pharmaceutical Institute to prepare for a career as a pharmacist. She took me along, but I soon found that this was not my line of study. My future was unsettled, but this did not prevent me from enjoying Berlin.

My friend Martin Wollner was studying law at the University of Berlin. He was glad to see me, but was flabbergasted when I told him of my adventure with a married man, and thoroughly disapproved of my egging Arnold along.

Nevertheless, we and his friends had much fun together. We frequented the little cafes and cabarets on the Kurfuersten-damm, saw controversial plays, and savored the hectic life in Berlin during the last year of the Weimar Republic, which was so masterfully recreated in the film "Cabaret." After the semester ended and Martin returned to Nuernberg, I spent much time with my cousins who said that they found my lifestyle disgusting, but secretly admired me. They did not have a circle of friends of both sexes as we had in our closely knit society. They were also still very innocent.

In 1932, Elfriede, the oldest of my cousins, was 22 years. She worked as a secretary in an office. She was a German-type beauty with deep blue eyes, shining blonde hair, and a peaches-and-cream complexion. As a teenager, she had had a bad spill from her bicycle and had suffered a serious concussion. Afterwards, she developed diabetes. She was able to control it with a strict diet, and she injected herself twice daily with insulin. Otherwise, she was able to lead a normal life and continue with her athletics and swimming. We used to go together to the large indoor swimming pool in the Lunapark after her work, and afterwards stroll through the amusement park or go to a dance hall where we danced with strangers, but never met with them afterwards.

Once, Elfriede invited me to go with her and her boyfriend on a hike through the sandy pine forests around Berlin, but I found their relationship tense and unnatural.

During one of our intimate conversations, Elfriede confessed shamefacedly, "You know, I have given myself once to a man." I answered in my matter-of-fact way, "At least it seems that you did not become pregnant." Elfriede was utterly disgusted, "What do you think of me? I merely let him kiss me, and kissed back." Elfriede was able to go to England soon after Hitler came to power. She worked, got married, suffered many miscarriages, and died later at a young age from tuberculosis.

Her youngest sister, Irene, went to a secretarial school. She was a shy, withdrawn girl who felt insignificant, overshadowed by her older sisters who got all the attention of parents and friends. She went to England with her older sister, and emigrated to America after Elfriede's death, having survived the London Blitz. She never married, but is leading a happy life in New York as personal secretary of a famous professor at Columbia University.

Elvira is the same age as I am. She was always a dreamer, living in a world of poetic imagination which I shared whenever we had a chance to be together, with me always dragging her back into everyday reality. We both love each other dearly, though our lives cross each other's only occasionally.

In 1932 she was working in the pharmacy of her Aunt Elli, the widow of Hans' brother who had inherited a prosperous pharmacy from her husband. Elvira had dropped out of high school because of the ever-growing anti-semitism, and Aunt

Elli invited her to work in the pharmacy. She also encouraged her to study pharmaceutics and to manage the pharmacy until her own children were old enough to take over. Elvira went to evening school and succeeded in passing the abitur. Then she enrolled as a part time student in the Institute of Pharmacology where I accompanied her a few times to her lectures. She introduced me to her friends and fellow students, some of whom came from Teheran.

Through her Iranian friends she learned about Persian culture and fell in love with it--not with her friends. The strange oriental country of their origin fascinated her. She studied Persian language and culture.

When her friends returned to Teheran at semester's end, they encouraged her to visit their homeland. She became obsessed with a desire to live in Persia, and finally decided to go there for a lengthy stay. Elvira's adventure took place before the great exodus of German Jews, when it was extremely unusual for a middle-class girl to visit a strange country on her own.

Toni and Hans remained in Germany after the Nazi takeover. Their three daughters, though, had all left the country by 1934. Hans did not expect to be persecuted. He was a German patriot, and had served his country in World War I. After the outbreak of World War II, Toni was forced by the government to work in an ammunitions factory. One day she did not return from work. A few days later a postcard arrived which said, "I was deported to Auschwitz. I am well." This was her last message.

Hans expected to be arrested after Toni's deportation. He decided to leave his home, and packed a knapsack with a few valuables, a change of clothes and a little food. But the next morning, before he had a chance to leave, the storm troopers knocked at his door. He shouted, "Wait until I have dressed," and jumped out of the window into the garden and over the fence. By the time the storm troopers had broken down the door, he was climbing the fence. They fired a few shots at him but missed. They searched the streets around his house, but could not find him because he was lying in a culvert.

He stayed there for a couple of days, then returned home one night, got his knapsack and walked for miles through the silent city into Grunewald, the forest surrounding Berlin. There he found refuge in a weekend cabin of German friends.

They found him there on the weekend and supplied him with food; however, he could not light a fire for fear he would arouse suspicion.

When winter came, his friends forged ration cards for him and he lived in different air raid shelters, returning to the forest in spring.

I do not know much more about his "underground years". It seems that he was not the only refugee in the forest, because many half-starved refugees who had survived in the forest surrendered to the liberating American army when they conquered Berlin.

Hans, who was very sick, was sent to a sanatorium in Switzerland to recover. He later joined his daughters in New York, where he enjoyed his granddaughter, wrote a book entitled "Never Again War" and died at the age of 83.

XXV. 1932 Vienna

As spring covered the shrubs in the garden with little buds, I grew morose. What should I do? I could not study in Berlin. I did not want to go back to Nuernberg, and my parents did not have enough money to send me to another university in Germany.

Martin was back in Nuernberg. My cousins and the Ludwig parents were busy. I had no friends of my own, except for distant relatives. I went halfheartedly to the museums and did some window shopping, reading and writing. I itched for action and involvement.

Then, one day, I received an electrifying letter from my father, who seldom wrote. He said that he had some money in Austria, but could not transfer it to Germany because of the Austrian law that no money could be taken out of the country. His agent had advised him to come himself to Austria and spend the money there. Would I like to go to Vienna and continue my studies?

I was absolutely delighted and lost no time in thanking him for his offer. I planned my trip to Vienna as a grand production in three days. First of all, I took advantage of a special rate for students on airplanes in Germany, and flew in a small six-seater plane to Dresden. I slept in the youth hostel and took a full day for sightseeing, including a visit to the famous Zwinger museum. In the evening I was able to see "The Egyptian Helen" by Richard Strauss in the beautiful, rococo opera house. I had an inexpensive seat high on the third balcony where it was very hot and, unfortunately, I fell asleep through part of the performance.

The next day, I took an early train to Prague where I went sightseeing until my feet could carry me no longer, and I rested in the old Jewish cemetery under trees in their springtime wedding gowns with old, half-buried tombstones around me. As it grew dark I went to the railway station, where I had some refreshments and sat in the waiting room until the departure of the night train to Vienna. I slept soundly from Prague to Vienna on the hard wooden bench of my compartment, with my suitcase as a pillow.

I left my luggage at the train station and went straight to the housing bureau of the university. I looked at the least expensive room they had to offer. It was in a nice neighborhood, near the Ringstrasse, not too far from the university, but it was small, and to get to the room I had to cross the living room of the landlord, which was not separated by a door but only by thick drapes. I knew that my funds were very limited, and rented the room right away.

Then I went back to the university, where I was able to enroll without any difficulties. I only registered for two lab courses in chemistry and physics, and one lecture in chemistry.

I had a few days before the start of the semester, during which I was very lonely yet exhilarated by spring, the mild weather, and the blooming trees and flowers. It was the time of lilac bloom, when all of Vienna was filled with its sweet aroma. I also enjoyed the wonderful coffeehouses of Vienna where the customers could sit for hours for the price of one cup of coffee, either inside or on the sidewalk, and read to their heart's content all the newspapers and magazines which were hanging on a rack in the lobby. I also visited Papa's agent and his pretty wife, distant relatives, who invited me for a Sunday dinner of Wiener Schnitzel and Viennese pastries, and afterwards to a show in a theater.

The last day of vacation I met a lady who roomed in the same house, but in a large, comfortable room with a private entrance from the hallway. Her name was Phyllis. She was divorced from her American husband and took courses in psychoanalysis at the university. She was also a journalist and had her own car, which was unusual. We had supper together and liked each other right away.

The first day of school arrived. I spent the morning at the chemistry lab, bought the necessary equipment, and met Heiner, a young Austrian farm boy who was also taking the class. We were assigned to the same table and would work together throughout the semester. We found out that we also took the same physical lab course. Heiner and I became good friends as time went by, and usually had our lunch together in the inexpensive students' restaurant.

After I finished my preliminary work at the lab, I went for lunch to a little open-air milk bar, opposite the main building of the university in the shadow of the Votive Church. I nearly keeled over when I saw my friend Arne sitting between two pretty girls, drinking milk. He was as surprised to see me as I was to see him. I joined him and his girls and no longer felt lonely.

Soon after the start of the semester was the long Pentecost weekend and five days of leisure. Phyllis and I went to the swimming pool in the Olympic stadium and met Arne and his satellites.

We talked about our plans for the coming vacation, and found out that none of us had ever been to Budapest. Phyllis offered to drive us there if we shared the expenses for gas. Early the next morning we were on our way along the Danube river, which got wider and bluer the further we got away from Vienna. As soon as we had crossed the border into Hungary we had an unforgettable meal of goulash and green wine in a rustic inn. Our spirits rose sky high. We sang and told jokes as we continued on our way until we had the first spectacular glimpse of Budapest, the parliament building at the bend of the river, and the dominating castle on top of a hill. We settled down at the youth hostel, drove back to

town, had a tour of the parliament building, and afterwards
enjoyed Hungarian goulash with gypsy music. Budapest was
the most beautiful town I had ever seen, except for my native
Nuernberg. The three days were a symphony of singing
violins, flowers, elegant spas, architectural delights, and
goulash. It was time to return, just as tensions arose among us
four girls for the attentions of our Adonis.

When we came back to Vienna, life settled into a pleasant
routine of work, swimming, theater and opera, and Sunday
hikes into the surrounding hills.

I explored Vienna on my own or with my lab partner Heiner,
with whom I had developed a satisfying friendship, and we
went together to museums and the Palace of Schoenbrunn,
but he never went with me to the theater; that bored him. I
took advantage of the inexpensive student tickets, standing
room only, in the opera and the Burgtheater, though I was
never able to see all the action because I could not stand very
long and had to sit down on the steps, listening with only an
occasional glance of the stage.

1932 was the last year of the relaxed Austrian way of life
before the "Anschluss," the reunion of Austria with Hitler's
Germany as one nation. The Austrians were still proud of
their "Schlendrian," a word that is hard to translate. It means
a leisurely laziness, a friendly pessimism, a sensuous enjoyment of life in the face of depression, a gentle resignation
with waltz music in the background. Vienna was an
overblown rose, a fading beauty basking in its past glory.

As time went by, I spent more of my free time with Heiner
and less time with Arne and company. During the middle of
the semester there was a student strike which shut down the
university for a number of days. I have not the slightest
recollection what it was about, but Heiner and I took advantage of the strike to take a trip.

We hitchhiked southward toward the Alps, and arrived at the Semmering Pass as the sun was low on the horizon. We walked along the highway, going up the mountain, but no car stopped for us. It got dark. We were hungry, tired, and far away from civilization. We fell down on a meadow at the wayside and fell asleep right away. Later, as it got cold, we both woke up and huddled together for warmth. But I told Heiner that I was a virgin and had no intention of changing that. Heiner answered with a sigh of relief, and said, "That's good. Then I don't have to be unfaithful to my Annamirl." We lay there quietly, looking at the stars, sleeping intermittently until dawn. We found a ride in the morning, went to a restaurant and had a good breakfast. We hiked until noon through the beautiful valley of the Murz River, and finally took a train back to Vienna.

One day, Phyllis came to my room and told me, "An old friend of mine has invited me to spend the weekend with him. He wants to go to a fabulous place, but I don't want to go to bed with him. Would you like to come along as my chaperone?" I said, "I don't think that he will agree to that, but ask him anyway whether he would go with the two of us."

Phyllis' beau agreed to my presence. He was a nobleman, and we would spend the night in his castle. The reason why he agreed was that he had to visit his castle, but had no car. He was a nice, well-educated man, and we had an animated conversation as we drove westward along the Danube river. We visited Stift Melk on the way, a monastery with one of the most beautiful Renaissance churches of Austria, high on a cliff, overlooking the river.

We had dinner with lots of wine and sat talking and drinking until late at night.

We were mellow and lightheaded when we drove in deep darkness over the drawbridge into the castle yard. Phyllis' friend opened the oaken door with a huge key, and led us through many dark rooms while we were holding on to him. Finally he stopped and lit a candle, bid us goodnight, and left us with the flickering candle in a cavernous room with two canopied four-poster beds. The beds had clean, fresh sheets. There was no washroom in sight, but we found chamber pots under the beds.

We both fell asleep right away. When I woke up, Phyllis was still fast asleep, and I went in search of a washroom. The room we were in was furnished in medieval style with faded tapestries and carved chests. In the next room, which was similarly furnished, a knight in shining armor stood guard. After the first shock, I found out that it was armor without a knight. I went through many rooms, all similarly furnished with collections of medieval arms and armor everywhere. Finally, I found an old woman who showed me a primitive bathroom, even brought me a pitcher with hot water, and showed me a sunny, friendly breakfast room where a table was set for the three of us.

When I found my way back to Phyllis, getting lost more than once on the way, I found Phyllis awake, laughing at my bewilderment.

At breakfast, they explained to me that this was a "Gschnassburg." I had no idea what a Gschnassburg was, and was told that it was a place where festivities continued during Mardi Gras after the ball was over. The old woman served us a hearty breakfast, but I was still speechless from the adventure and the wonders of this enchanted castle.

The semester drew to its close. Phyllis would leave Vienna to go to Switzerland. She invited me to share the ride to Munich, and take the train from there.

We had a wonderful trip through the Austrian Alps. We visited Salzburg and I arrived home full of memories of a beautiful summer.

The Nazis in Nuernberg in 1933.

XXVI. The Fateful Year 1933

While I was in Vienna, I lived suspended in a shell, completely absorbed in my personal life, with no interest in politics or social problems.

As soon as I returned to Erlangen for school I got caught in the mainstream of politics. Nazis were marching in the streets with their swastika banners, shouting anti-Jewish slogans at the top of their voices. When they were not marching in their brown shirts or black shirts, they had bloody confrontations in the streets with activist members of the Communist party.

We watched with fear and despair the steamroller effect of Nazi propaganda. The Reichstag was unable to form a coalition government of center and moderate left-wing parties. One chancellor after another had to resign, and call for new elections. Each election brought more votes for the radical parties on each end of the spectrum, the Nazis on the right, and the communists on the left. The Nazis gathered about 30 or more percent of the votes, while the communists got nearly 20 percent. Social Democrats, the majority party throughout most of the years of the Weimar Republic, with all the other parties, were short of a majority. In 1932, General Field Marshall Hindenburg had won the presidency against Hitler, with the help of all parties except communists and Nazis. Now, the Field Marshall was forced to appoint his former opponent to the far more powerful position of Reichskanzler--Chancellor--and entrust him with the task of forming a coalition government of right-wing parties, a government in which the Nazis held only three of the 11 cabinet seats. This was not enough for Hitler. He therefore called for new elections in March 1933.

To combat the tide of the Nazis, all anti-Hitler parties formed the "Eiserne Front" the iron front. All my friends had joined this group, and we formed a student club in Erlangen that included Catholics as well as communists. It was a motley collection of individuals that were only united by their opposition to Hitler. We had an office in Erlangen where our records were kept, but I was so little active that I never visited this office.

I was happy to resume my studies for my fifth semester, in which I planned to finish the required work in inorganic chemistry. In the lab, I worked in partnership with Elisabeth, a Catholic girl from Bamberg, a city north of Erlangen. Our helper and protector was Leonhard Birkhofer, who had shown a special interest in me from the beginning, and who was happy that I had returned.

Leonhard was a thin man with a sallow complexion. He had short-clipped black hair, close-set eyes, and a huge beak of a nose in his narrow face.

He was aware of his lack of sex appeal and, therefore he was very shy. It was only his pity for me when I was not invited to the Christmas party of the chemistry lab the previous year that made him bold enough to invite me. But, since then, an easy friendship had sprung up between us. I greatly appreciated the delicious liqueurs that he concocted with the duty-free alcohol that he requisitioned for his experiments. Finally, he fell in love with me while I felt only friendship for him. Leonhard was solely interested in science and had no desire to get involved in politics, social problems, or cultural interests. He also never spoke about his personal life or his family. We might go to a movie together, but he declined to go with me to a concert, a play, or to the opera. Because of this, our relationship was mostly confined to the nitty-gritty of daily encounters in the lab, and one memorable visit to Elisabeth's family in Bamberg.

But it seemed that he speculated about my life outside the lab, and one day he related a dream that he purported to have had.

He said that he was together with the other assistants, and each of them put his hand over fumes of nitric acid. If his girlfriend was a virgin, the acid would not affect his hand. If she was no virgin, his hand would turn yellow.

"What happened to your hand?" I asked him.

"I didn't put it out. I chickened out."

My reply was truthful, "You could have put out your hand." But I think he did not believe me.

I took the same train to Erlangen every morning with a Jewish girlfriend. She whistled in front of my house, and I joined her. We rode with her colleagues, and talked about our studies and trivia, but never about politics because we were afraid somebody might overhear us. That our group consisted of Jews and non-Jews was telling enough. Leonhard boarded the same train in Fuerth, the next station. He usually went to a different car because he was too shy, or did not care for our company. He also refused to join the anti-Hitler student club.

In the afternoon, I took a different train every day. I preferred to ride alone because this was my sacred study time. One day each week I ate a lonely supper in the student cafeteria when I caught up with my written work, and went later to the gym for exercise. There, I met some of my former schoolmates who also studied in Erlangen. They showed pleasure in meeting me, but avoided talking to me in public. I suspected that they were members of the Nazi party and were embarrassed to show their friendship with me. After a few months, I dropped out of the physical educational class and never heard from my former classmates again.

One other Jew worked with me in the chemical lab. He was also a member of the anti-Hitler student club. Robert Heller was from Nuernberg, and I knew him well because he had been a member of the Tanzstunde but he had no friends other than me in the lab, and was rather isolated.

During this period of my life I rarely saw my family, except occasionally at the dinner table. My brother Floh had been sent to Wyk auf Foehr, the same island in the North Sea where I had spent a summer. He was also sent there for health reasons because he was so small and underweight for his age, and the salty, clean air of the island was supposed to stimulate his appetite. He was working as an apprentice to a business friend of my father who produced quality furniture in his carpentry shop. I had little rapport with Heinz and Werner who were still in high school and busy in the Kameraden, a group that still rejected Zionism.

Most of the my evenings were devoted to Zionist activities. My plans were to emigrate to Palestine, or Erez Israel as we called it during the time of the British Mandate, after I had finished my studies.

The British government of Palestine had issued the Balfour Declaration after World War I, promising to establish a Jewish cultural center in the country and encourage Jewish immigration without infringing on the rights of the native Arab population or the representatives of the Christian establishments. It was an impossible dream because the Arabs strongly objected to Jewish immigration. A compromise was worked out in which Jewish capitalists with at least 1,000 British pounds (approximately $5000 in 1932) were allowed to enter the country as immigrants, while only a limited number of certificates for persons without means were given to the Jewish agency to distribute according to their discretion. These cherished certificates were given to people who had been trained to be farmers or craftsmen, because the Jewish Agency was interested in buying land from the Arabs through the Jewish National Fund, and let Jews work on it. The organization which prepared young people in agriculture was called the Hechaluz, the pioneers.

The older, wealthier members of the Zionistic organization did not actually plan to emigrate at this point, but they contributed generously to the Jewish National Fund which bought the land and planted forests, and the Keren Kajemeth, the fund that paid for the establishment of Jewish colonies, schools and hospitals. Other Jewish organizations also contributed to needs of the Jewish population in Palestine.

Our local group had an office to collect money, to arrange activities, and to help the young people who were preparing for their emigration. We had Hebrew courses, courses in Jewish history, and the history of Zionism. Jews from Eastern Europe, where they had been persecuted, had gone to Palestine since the beginning of the century and had established settlements, but only after Theodor Herzl, an Austrian Jew, had promoted a "Jewish State", did the Zionist movement include Western Jews. Only 200,000 Jews were living in Palestine in 1933.

I belonged to the Young Zionists, a group that was engaged in social activities like dancing, but my heart was with the Hechaluz. The members of the Hechaluz in Nuernberg had built a ramshackle house with their own hand about 10 miles south of the city. The house was shelter for members who tended the surrounding garden and fields. Other members lived, commune style, in a rented flat in Nuernberg, as apprentices for various trades. Most of the Chaluzim, the pioneers, were Ostjuden, people who had come from Russia or Poland, or other East European countries after W.W.I. Generally, they were poorer and less educated than the German city Jews, who still had a long way to go before they got their hands dirty.

My friends and I often joined the Chaluzim on Sundays in their house, where we had picnics and danced the hora, the Jewish national dance, until we were exhausted.

We used to hike the five miles from the last streetcar station marching in formation, as the Germans liked to do. One Sunday evening, on our return after a satisfying day with the

Chaluzim, we were marching and singing Hebrew words to a German song when we came through a village. In the market place we found a division of brown-shirted storm troopers performing military exercises to which they shouted, again and again, "Judah verrecke!"--a miserable death to the Jews. We were deeply shaken and continued to walk silently in small groups, never marching in formation again.

Though the situation in Germany worsened from day to day, nothing could prevent the Germans from celebrating the "Fashing," the prelenten period of revelry and carousing. The most brilliant affairs were the lavish masked balls in one of the theaters. This was the first year that my parents allowed me to attend these official dances.

My cousin Albert Rosenfelder and his non-Jewish wife, Tini, invited me to go with them. Tini and I had matching costumes, and went full of anticipation. At first I sat sedately with my relatives until I found a student from the university who introduced me to his friends, a lively group of fans of a beloved actress of the municipal theater, Jutta Versen. We drank champagne at a table on the first balcony where we could admire the dancing and the fancy costumes, as well as the lavish decorations. We danced, sang, flirted, and kissed each other slyly on the backstairs of the theater.

When the party was over, we asked for the bill. We all contributed whatever money we had, but it was not enough to pay for all the champagne. One of the group had to give his golden watch as security to the waiter. Nevertheless, at 2:00 a.m. we were still full of pep, and nobody wanted to go home. We all went together to the Ratskeller, a restaurant that catered for after-the-ball parties, and drank beer and ate sausages, and continued to enjoy ourselves.

At daybreak I knew that I had to go home and face the music, reproaches that I had left my chaperones without a word, and nobody knew where I was. Jutta and the whole bunch went home with me to help me weather the storm. My mother, who had to get out of bed, was a great sport. She was so flattered by the visit of the famous actress that she forgot to blame me and made coffee for us, even producing sweet rolls out of nowhere.

My partner during the evening, who was partly Jewish, a descendant of the famous Jewish philosopher Moses Mendelsohn, and of the even more famous composer Felix Mendelsohn, suggested that we all accompany him to Erlangen, and continue the feast in his house.

We took the next train, ate again, walked in the park, and ended up in Erlangen's famous Cafe Mengin.

My parents were by now worried about their wayward daughter, and came by car to Erlangen where they found all of us in the cafe. They were graciously accepted, and introduced to everyone. At last, I went quietly and willingly home with them because I was tired.

During the rest of the Fashing, my newly found friends and I went to many parties in Erlangen and Nuernberg. The highlight was an artist's party in Jutta's house, where several young actors and actresses performed for us. The last great party was again in the Apollo Theater. It was the Rosenmontag Gala on February 26, on the eve of Shrove Tuesday. We were blissfully happy at the moment when we heard the sobering news that the Reichstag, the German parliament building, was on fire.

A dazed man who said that his name was Luebke and that he was a communist was found in the basement of the building with incendiary material in his hands. It was just one week before the elections. Hitler proclaimed that the communists had burned the Reichstag, and outlawed the communist party. Many of its leaders were arrested, and the party was taken off the ballot. Without the communist vote, Hitler got a clear

majority and declared himself the "Fuehrer," the dictator of
the Third Reich.

Luebke was quickly executed, and only much later the truth
came out that he was put there by Hitler's henchmen through
an underground passage, that he was a deranged person but
no communist, and the pieces of the puzzle--how he was so
quickly found and other incongruities, fell into place.

Hitler lost no time in fulfilling his campaign promise to
persecute the Jews. Jewish government employees, Jewish
teachers and judges were immediately dismissed, and on May
2nd of 1933 a nationwide boycott of Jewish establishments
was ordered. Storm troopers guarded the entrances of Jewish
retail stores, doctors' and lawyers' offices. They were not
allowed to use force, but had to convince patrons that people
who did business with Jews were traitors and enemies of the
people. Most people were intimidated, and docilely obeyed.

My friends and I had assembled in the millinery store of our
friend Max. From there we went from one Jewish store to the
other, defying the guards, and comforting the dazed owners.
Finally we returned to Max's store and compared notes. That
day we realized our hopeless situation as a hated and
persecuted minority, though we were still unaware of the
coming disaster.

After closing time we went home with Max for supper and a
musical soiree. Max and Arne played music of the great German composers on the piano, and Annamarie sang Lieder by
Schubert, Hugo Wolf and Mahler until tears rolled down our
cheeks.

It was our swan song. We never had another musical evening.
All of us left Germany during the next year.

———————●———————

XXVII. The First Year Of The Third Reich

After Hitler's great victory at the polls, changes took place that affected every German citizen. One of the first moves of the new government was to introduce the draft. Within a few weeks, the streets were cleared of young, unemployed men. The older unemployed people soon found work in the production of war material, or building new freeways, the "Autobahnen." Together with work for everyone, Hitler introduced a great program called "Kraft durch Freude," Strength through Joy. This program provided vacations for workers, mothers and children. Ships were chartered for fabulous cruises, vacation camps were built for families, bicycle tours through the most picturesque parts of Germany were arranged, until the last of the people had lived through one or more unforgettable weeks of relaxation and enjoyment.

The mood in Germany changed completely during the summer of 1933, and even former skeptics were convinced that Hitler had the good of his people at heart.

There was an undercurrent of despair by the families of the arrested, "enemies of the people", the leaders of opposition parties, or simply, people who had spoken out against the dictator about the loss of democracy, but their complaints were drowned in the wave of euphoria. The severely censored newspapers carried only praise for the Fuehrer's achievements, and every voice of dissent was silenced. Hitler could do no wrong, and the German people wholeheartedly applauded his actions against left-wing leaders, dissenting clergy, and, of course, the "profiteering" Jews.

Our family's problems started within weeks of the great official boycott of Jewish establishments. Germans still went shopping in Jewish stores and visited Jewish lawyers and physicians, but nobody dared to make major purchases that would be delivered to their house in a van of a Jewish store in full view of their suspicious neighbors.

Papa's business was dead within a month, and he had to stop payments to his creditors. Again, bankruptcy loomed on the horizon. His Ottensooser relatives, who were also his bankers, came to his rescue and let his debt ride, which gave Papa the opportunity to come to an agreement with his other creditors. He sold his large factory for a pittance to an ardent Nazi, and kept only a small workshop that he had recently acquired.

Papa became despondent and brooded over means of suicide that would look like an accident so that his family and relatives could cash in on his life insurance. He mulled over his intention and informed every member of the family how he would save them through his forthcoming death. We were very worried about him.

The Jewish congregation informed me that my scholarship had to be cancelled because all the available funds had to be used in vocational training of would-be emigrants, and to send children abroad.

I still went to Erlangen because I wanted to complete at least the first part of my studies and pass the first comprehensive chemistry examination. It was of utmost importance to pass this test because no credits were given for any course without it. I had no chance to continue my studies anywhere in the world unless I passed this test.

I was as depressed and preoccupied as all my friends, and so it happened that I missed my morning train for the first time during all the years in Erlangen. As soon as I arrived at the lab my instructor came to me and said, "How lucky that you are late, Fraulein Braun. The Gestapo has just left. They were looking for you and Heller, and took Heller with them." I returned home on the next train. After many phone calls, I learned that all headquarters of anti-Hitler student clubs throughout the nation had been raided the day before, and warrants for the arrest of all members had been issued.

Friends who studied at universities out of town and who escaped arrest had come back to Nuernberg. We all met the same evening. They decided to leave Germany the same night, with just a backpack, over mountain trails into Switzerland.

Georg Josephthal, Martin Wollner and many friends left with this group, but I did not go with them because I could not leave my family in this time of crisis. After a restless night, the bell rang early the next morning. I was apprehensive because I was afraid that the Gestapo had caught up with me. But it was Leonhard who said that he had arranged with the department head that I could take my test within a week. He would coach me, get all the necessary signatures, and I could go to Erlangen one more time to take the oral test in front of a consortium of professors in order to get all the credit for five semesters of chemistry.

I kissed him and thanked him with all my heart, and we sat down right away for my first session of concentrated review of all the material I had to know for the test.

I was lost to the outside world during the next week. Leonhard also did not go to Erlangen, but came everyday to drill me. On the appointed day, Leonhard went with me to Erlangen, and sat with crossed fingers behind the closed door of the examination room while I faced the examination board with trembling and fear. I passed with flying colors. We returned to Nuernberg in the early afternoon.

I went home only to tell my family the good news, then continued on to go to the mother of a friend who had a diploma in home economics. I asked her whether she would like to teach me cooking and homemaking because I thought that I had to keep busy and learn something practical.

She agreed readily, under the condition that I find a group of four or five students to form a class. I knew that there were other displaced students like me who would welcome this opportunity. I went to the Jewish youth home and put up a notice. From there I went to the Zionist office to see if I could find companions for the course.

The secretary knew of nobody offhand, but told me that she was going to Israel, and asked whether I knew anybody to take her place. I said that I would be delighted to take the job.

I soon found four other students for the home economics course, and for the following month I studied cooking, ironing, house cleaning, and shopping in the mornings, and typing in the afternoons.

I was never able to master touch typing, but I became a great cook and even learned to cook according to the Jewish dietary laws. It turned out that these lessons were more beneficial in my future life than my chemistry and science studies, and while my textbooks and my collection of zoological microscopic slides got lost during my future wanderings, the stained and dogeared cookbook that I wrote in this class is still with me.

A month later, I started work as secretary of the Jewish National Fund for northern Bavaria. A week later, the other girl in the office in charge of local affairs also left to go to Israel, and I took over her responsibilities in addition to the job for which I was originally hired. I was able to do this because I had a large number of volunteers. In the mornings I sat at either of the large desks, reading and answering the mail, and keeping the books and files. In the afternoons, I supervised my little army of volunteers to send out invitations and leaflets, and sent them with the giftbook to families, asking them to give money to plant trees in Erez Israel in lieu of presents on occasions like bar mitzvahs, anniversaries or birthdays, and in memory of deceased friends or relatives. My helpers also distributed and emptied the ubiquitous little blue savings boxes of the Kerem Kajemeth, the Jewish National Fund. Many Jewish homes already had such blue boxes with the star of David printed on them, and as more and more Jews thought of Palestine as a source of escape, we were able to place the boxes in nearly every Jewish home. From time to time, I closed my office for a few days to take care of the boxes in other communities in the vicinity. A lot of money passed through my hands.

In the evenings I organized meetings and Hebrew classes. Nevertheless, I suffered from gloom at home where Papa had nothing to do but to worry.

One day a letter arrived in the mail from a large Jewish travel agency in Berlin. They asked us to find an agent for them in our area to sell steamship tickets to emigrants. I asked the president of our organization to recommend my father for this job. Papa was delighted. He revived. After a short training period in Berlin, he set up an office in a room that a Jewish shipping agency gave him free of charge on the condition that he recommend their shipping agency to his clients. Papa, who liked to organize new enterprises, had the idea of building shipping containers for his clients in the remnants of his factory. Papa's business became a great success, and gave him the opportunity to travel to prospective customers all over northern Bavaria to measure their belongings for the size of the necessary containers. Mama was his steady companion on his trips, and their married life took on new meaning. During 1933 and 1934, Jews were still able to leave Germany without restrictions.

One evening, while the rest of the family was out, I had a meeting of the W.I.Z.O., the Jewish Women's Organization in our house. Suddenly, the bell rang loud and persistently. When I opened the door I was confronted by a group of about 15 sinister-looking brown-shirts. They said they had heard that an illegal assembly was going on in our house. Their leader took the names of the women in attendance while the rest of them swarmed all over our apartment. They searched the bookcase for subversive literature and took some of the books away. At last everyone was allowed to leave, except the chairwoman and me. We were marched through the dark streets to the police station, surrounded by the stern-looking storm troopers. Fortunately, at the police station the brown-shirts had no authority and the police officers were friendly and polite. They told us that a permit was necessary for every meeting previous to the event. After we had promised to get a permit for all our future meetings, we were told to go home.

It was the last meeting in my beautiful green room in the Sandstrasse.

Though my father again had a regular income, the expenses of the household had to be cut down. Maria, who was now more a friend than a servant, knew that her days in our household were numbered. She answered an ad in a Catholic publication in which a widower, owner of a butcher shop, was looking for a wife. Mr. Butcher replied that he was interested, and Maria and Mama traveled together to his place in Thuringia. They liked what they saw. Maria left us to become the wife of a very fat old man and co-owner of the butcher shop, in which she invested all her savings. It was not to be a happy ending because she had to work very hard, became sick, and died soon. But, at least for a few years, she enjoyed her new status as the butcher's wife.

We gave up the apartment in the Sandstrasse, and moved to a much smaller apartment on the outskirts of the city. Mama, who hated to cook all her life, had to cook for us, and had the help of a Jewish woman for only a few hours on weekdays for cleaning. It turned out that Mama was an excellent cook and her concoctions were far superior to the humdrum fare that Maria had provided for us.

Not all of our friends were as lucky as I was on the day the Gestapo rounded up the members of the student club. They arrested a number of people that we knew and sent them to the infamous concentration camp in Dachau. One day, two families in Nuernberg received sealed coffins with the remains of their sons. An accompanying letter said that they were shot while trying to escape, and they were ordered not to open the coffins. One of the families opened the coffin and saw the mutilated body of their son with a bullet wound in his chest. All the other young men from Nuernberg who had been sent to Dachau were killed before the beginning of World War II. Only one of them, my friend Hugo Burkhard, with whom we used to ride on the train from the Ludwigshoehe to Nuernberg long ago, was set free. He wrote a book, "Tanz Mal Jude", *Dance Jew*, about the unspeakable atrocities that he and other inmates had suffered during their years in Dachau. I read the book with tears in my eyes and had to lay it down many times because it was so unbelievably sad. I wrote to the publisher for Hugo's address, but he was dead before my letter reached him.

All restaurants in Nuernberg bore a sign, "Jews are not welcome," and we no longer went out to eat or sit in coffeehouses. We were also banned from the theaters and the opera. But one day the president of the Zionist organization and I had to prepare for a meeting. He invited me to have dinner with him after work before the meeting. The only restaurant without the demeaning sign was in the railway station. Nuernberg was a railway center where railway lines from all over Germany met the Orient Express from Paris to Istanbul. The Nazis did not want to shock foreign visitors with their anti-Semitic policies by openly displaying the anti-

Jewish sign. We had an excellent dinner and afterwards, still in the restaurant, we compared notes and I showed him the correspondence that was to be read at the meeting. We were deeply immersed in our activities when two plainclothes policemen approached our table and displayed their badges. They said, "You are under arrest."

They explained that they had watched us for awhile and seen that we exchanged letters with foreign postage stamps, and they suspected that we were spies. We were escorted to the police station where we were interrogated separately at great length until they were satisfied that our letters from emigrants to Palestine were completely harmless.

The members at the meeting were anxiously waiting for us, sensing that something had gone wrong. We both were limp after our ordeal was over, but happy to reassure our friends that nothing was wrong.

As the year went on, one after the other of our friends left Germany. At that time it was still easy to obtain a passport because the civil administration was headed by the old bureaucracy. Only a few years later the passports of all Jews were stamped with a yellow "J" for Jew, and all male Jews had to take the middle name Israel, and all Jewish women bore the middle name "Sarah." Most of the people of my generation were able to escape because we had no property that we were unwilling to leave behind, nor were we so young that we were dependent on our parents. Many parents sent their children to Jewish schools in England or the United States. The British authorities issued special permits for young people to go to school in Palestine which were not counted towards the regular quota. Jews all over the world contributed money for this "Youth Aliyah." Aliyah is the Hebrew word for ascend, and we used this word for immigration to Erez Israel, the land of Israel that was not yet a Jewish state.

I was already 22 years old, but I applied anyway for a permit to go as a student to a "Meshek Poaloth," a Jewish agricultural school in Palestine for girls. It was a school where I had to pay tuition and my own passage. This was no problem, because I was able to save my earnings since I did not have to help my family anymore.

I spent much of my free time helping Mama with household chores and shopping. One Saturday morning when I returned home from shopping, I found Mama very upset. She said that she had a phone call from the police who wanted to conduct a search of our office, and I had to return immediately to open the door for them. I took my bike and rode there. When I arrived they had already opened the door with a passkey. Four plainclothes policemen had thrown all our files on the floor and emptied the contents of all the drawers. They did not tell me what they were looking for, and left with a number of our records soon after my arrival.

I found out the reason for the search 45 years later. When I returned to Nuernberg I ordered a book published by the Municipal Library of Nuernberg, "The History of the Jews in Nuernberg (1146-1935)". When I received the book several months later, the first thing I did was look up in the index under the name "Braun." There I found an excerpt from a police report showing that the Nazis even violated the privacy of mail by opening and using private letters. They said that the police were opening the mail of Fraulein Braun, the Director of the Zionist Office, because she was suspected of illegally collecting money for this organization. It said that she had to be watched closely and that all the money had to be confiscated.

They could not find any money, because I had sent it the day before to our central office in Berlin, but they would have come back. In the report, they even mentioned that I was in charge of emptying the blue collection boxes that I described earlier.

I convinced my parents that I wanted to leave Nuernberg without waiting for my acceptance in the agricultural school. I called Mr. Nussbaum, a Jewish farmer in Wurtemberg, who took young Jewish people as apprentices in agriculture. I had dealt with him before, placing people from Nuernberg on his farm. I told him that my life was in danger, and begged him to accept me immediately.

He agreed, and his wife was delighted to have a servant girl in her house. I never saw the outside of the house or farm, because she kept me busy from morning till night. I had to get up before the rest of the family, light the fire in the huge kitchen stove, and prepare breakfast for the family and workers. Then she had me clean the house, wash clothes by hand on the washboard, and wash all the dishes. I had one hour of rest in the afternoon, during which I slept, and in the evening I fell into bed as soon as I had finished washing the dishes.

At last I collapsed with asthma and a bad back, and had to see the doctor. He phoned Mrs. Nussbaum and told her that my body was not able to perform such hard work, and that I had to take it easier. My duties had to be reduced, and as a token of the promise to teach me agriculture, I was ordered to dig the vegetable garden, and to cut cabbage for sauerkraut. My ordeal ended after five weeks, when I was accepted by the Meshek Poaloth. I did not give notice, but left on the earliest train, though my departure for Palestine was still two weeks away.

However, the Nussbaums did me a far-reaching favor. They paid my contributions to social security. After the war, a law was passed in Germany that all people who had worked a minimum of nine months in Germany, paid into the pension plan, but had to leave their work because of political persecution, were automatically given full credit until after the war, when they could have returned to Germany.

I had a lawyer working for me in Germany to find my records. He wrote back that he had found my contributions for my work at the Zionist office which was not enough to qualify for a pension, but that I had worked for a Mr. Nussbaum in Nueringen for a few weeks in 1934. He was able to find proof of the contributions, and I fulfilled the absolute minimum requirements to be eligible for a pension from Germany, which is now a welcome addition to my retirement income.

I stayed in Nuernberg only long enough to pack my belongings, and left a week before my departure from Trieste. My mother was heartbroken because she was afraid that she would never see me again. I did not share her sorrow, but looked forward to an exciting experience. I celebrated a joyous farewell from Europe by sightseeing in Zurich, Lugano, Milano, and Venice before meeting my future colleagues in the Jewish emigration hostel in Trieste. We boarded the SS Gerusalemme of the Lloyd Triestino Line the last week of April. Though we traveled third class, and though the sea was rough and we were all seasick part of the time, we enjoyed the voyage immensely, making new friends, trying to speak Hebrew, and dancing the horah.

We arrived in Jaffa on April 30, 1934, slept the first night in Tel Aviv, and on May Day we took the bus to Afuleh in the Emek Jesreel, our new home. When we arrived, we had no time to freshen up or unpack, but were driven in a horse-drawn wagon to a nearby kibbutz to celebrate the day of labor, and our arrival in the Promised Land.

XXVIII. End Of An Era

My mother's apartment in Jerusalem was the center of our family. The family was not only comprised of her children, grandchildren and greatgrandchildren, but cousins, nieces and nephews, many times removed, and friends who had adopted her as their mother. Before blindness prevented her from writing, her correspondence covered all five continents to which the family had dispersed after the exodus from Germany.

When Mother grew old and required around the clock nursing care, her sons, especially her daughter-in-law Gerda, devised a complicated schedule in which her relatives and friends, as well as paid help, shared in her care, so that she was able to stay in her own home instead of living in a nursing home, until she died at the blessed age of 94.

"Oma", a tender form of the German word for grandmother, as we all called her, had a bottomless capacity for giving and receiving love. She had the gift of listening with sympathy, understanding, and support. One of her friends called her "my own private Wailing Wall." Another of her regular visitors told me, "I have two old aunts whom I visit occasionally. When I visit my other aunt, she greets me reproachfully, 'So, you finally remembered my address.' When I visit your mother, her face lights up and she says, 'How nice of you to remember me.' "

Oma used to sit in her armchair and treat her frequent visitors to coffee, cake and an open ear. Some of them read to her, or did crossword puzzles with her, giving her the clues to which she gave the answers with lightning speed. But most of them poured out to her their tales of woe to get sympathy, consolation, and very little advice.

We, and all the family, pitched in to enable us in America to visit her frequently. It is a source of great joy to me that all our children and grandchildren knew her personally and loved her. I, myself, was able to visit her 15 times in the last 20 years.

When Jacob and I arrived on schedule in May of 1981 for a visit in Jerusalem, Oma had been admitted to the hospital the day before our arrival. My brother Floh told me she was confused and probably didn't know where she was. I went to the hospital right away. She recognized her "Stefferle" and said, "I wanted to be so enthusiastically happy with your visit, but now I cannot even feel joy." She also asked whether we were staying in her empty apartment and said, feeling my hands, "I am happy that your hands are soft. During your first years in Israel they were so hard with calluses." She also asked about our children, but dropped off to sleep before I could answer.

I stayed two days at her bedside and suffered agonies when I heard her wild cries, while she received painful treatment. I tried to feed her and give her liquids, but she did not want to eat or drink, and her mind was wandering. She was like a tiny, obstinate child.

On my last day with her, her blind eyes seemed to become clear and focused. Her doctors said, "I think your mother is seeing heaven already." Oma regarded me with clear, open eyes. I asked, "Can you see me?" She nodded and stared interestedly at the ceiling. "Do you see beautiful things?" I asked. She answered, faintly, "Yes, I can open my eyes again." I was not sure whether she had understood me and asked, "Can you move your fingers?" She instantly wiggled her fingers in my hand. I kissed her tenderly. She was peaceful now because the doctors had stopped treatment and let her rest. It seemed as if her condition had improved and she even took some nourishment.

So, we decided that I could go with Jacob and our friends on a trip to the Galilee. On the second day of our trip, while we were having lunch in a nice restaurant, overlooking the

Mediterranean, Jacob said suddenly, "We have to go back to Jerusalem right away."

When we arrived, Oma had been dead for a few hours. We were in my brother's house in the middle of frantic activities. In Israel, the dead are buried the same day or the day after death. Funeral arrangements had to be made, announcements had to be posted on bulletin boards throughout the city and in next day's papers, phone calls had to be made to friends and relatives throughout the country and to America.

The funeral was the following day at 3 p.m. The funeral is of stark simplicity because according to Jewish belief, all people are equal in death. The corpse is wrapped in a simple shroud and put on a bier without flowers or wreaths. The near relatives tear their clothes to express their mourning. Prayers are said in the funeral hall. Then the mourners proceed to the cemetery. A bus was provided for those without cars, the rest followed in their private cars in a long cortege.

The cemetery is on a beautifully landscaped hill with a splendid view over the mountains and valleys of Judea. Each tombstone is identical, a huge limestone slab on the floor with an inscription. No flowers are on the tombs. Visitors leave a pebble on the tombstone as a sign of their remembrance. Birds are singing in the trees. No other noise disturbs their concert.

Mother's grave, beside father's, was already dug. When we arrived, the gravediggers lined its bottom and side with thin limestone slabs, building a tiny room. Then they lowered the body into this little nest and covered it with a large slab of stone. Prayers were said, and then her sons, and later all the mourners filled the tomb with earth.

Nearly all of the about 150 people with us went to Oma's house, filling it to overflowing. According to Jewish custom, the nearest relatives, parents, children, brothers and sisters stay for one week in the house of the deceased, sitting on low stools, remembering his or her life, and receiving visitors. My brothers and I did not sit on low stools, and I did not say the traditional prayers, but we were in Oma's house for a full week.

During the week of the "Shiffe" we did not mourn for our mother. She had her long deserved peace, after a long life of sorrows and joys. Guests came and went. We talked about our parents and ourselves, and about the problem of Israel. Whenever there was a lull, we looked at old photographs that Oma had collected, reminisced about our childhood and later life. When the conversation with visitors was in Hebrew that I couldn't understand, I read old letters and diaries that Oma had preserved. We mourners were not allowed to be hosts to our guests. Oma's live-in companion was a graceful hostess.

I had an opportunity to meet all my friends and relatives in Israel, and to get to know my nephews and nieces better than ever before. They all were interested in the photos, and listened with great interest to our stories about them.

On the eighth day after Oma's death, the family went to the cemetery for traditional prayer, and afterwards each of us went again about his daily life and work.

Our matriarch was gone, we were no longer her children, but heads of our own growing families. An era in our family had come to its end.

GLOSSARY OF GERMAN TERMS

Abitur: The test in German High School after the 13th year, which corresponds to a Bachelor degree in an American college and is the entrance exam for University.

Anschluss: Invasion of Austria by Hitler to unite it with the German Reich.

Autobahn: Freeway.

Blau-Weiss: Blue and white, the colors of the Israeli flag, and the name of a Zionist youth organization.

Bund Deutscher Maedchen: A German youth organization for girls, later a Nazi organization.

Burschenschaften: An organization of German university students, founded by patriots in 1848. Later degenerated into fraternities whose main activities were drinking beer and fighting duels. Most of these students became Nazis.

Das Einjaehrige: Test taken by German students after the 10th year of high school. During the time of the German Empire, students who had passed this test had to serve only one year in the army; those who did not pass this test had to serve for three years. The name "Das Einjaehrige" was used even after World War I, when the draft was abolished.

Eiserne Front: The Iron Front, the merging of all anti-Hitler parties into a united front at the beginning of and shortly before the Hitler years.

Fasching: Mardi Gras. The time from January until Ash Wednesday.

Gschnasburg: A Viennese term for a castle, where young revelers spent the night after a Mardi Gras celebration.

Hausfreund: A friend of the family the term is used especially for single young men who were invited into middle class families with young daughters to enable young people of both sexes to mingle under strict supervision.

Herrenzimmer: The room for the man of the house. A library.

Hochzeitszeitung: Funny imitation of a newspaper, written especially for a wedding. It has news articles, ads and comments about the newlyweds, their families and friends.

Hoehere Maedchenschule: A high school for girls whose families could pay tuition.

Hundekarte: A railway ticket for dogs who could travel in the coaches with their masters.

Judischer Jugendbund: An organization for Jewish high school students.

Jugenstill: Art Nouveau.

Jungferntag: Meeting of married women who pretend to be unmarried and can have fun.

Kaffeeklatsch: Meeting of women for afternoon coffee and gossip.

Kameraden: A Jewish youth organization which copied the German organization "Der Wandervogel". Its members believed that the Jews could assimilate into German culture but retain their Jewish identity.

Kermess: The anniversary of a Church's saint, celebrated by a special service and carnival.

Kraft durch Freude: The institution by Hitler of a paid vacation for all German citizens, including women and children, with free trips or stays in a resort.

Meistersinger: Opera by Richard Wagner about an organization of craftsmen in Germany during the late Middle Ages whose members composed and sang music. Hans Sachs, a shoemaker and poet from Nuernberg, is the hero of the opera.

Oberrealschule: A type of German high school that did not teach Latin, as in the gymnasium, but concentrated its curriculum on science and modern languages. This school also led to the abitur.

Ostjuden: Jews who came to Germany from Eastern Europe, especially Russia, Poland and Lithuania.

Realschule: German high school that ended with the 10th grade and the "Einjaehrige" that taught science and modern languages.

Reichskanzler: Prime minister.

Saupreusse: Prussian pig, a term used by Bavarians who did not like the Prussians.

Schlagrahmdampfer: Whipped cream steamboat. This was an excursion boat on the Donau Main Canal in Nuernberg whose destination was a restaurant that served rich tortes with whipped cream.

Tanzstunde: A group of about 10-12 couples who took instruction in ballroom dancing and had many parties together.

Verein fuer den Klassischen chorgesang: A choir who performed at concerts of classical music. The members paid a membership fee. Only soloists got paid.

Wandervogel: A German youth organization that hiked throughout Germany and was deeply patriotic, shunning alcohol, smoking and ballroom dancing.

GLOSSARY OF HEBREW TERMS

Adonai he hoelohim: The Lord is God, the words which end the religious service on Yom Kippur.

Afikomen: A piece of matzah that the celebrant puts aside during the Seder, the celebration of the passover, for later use after dinner. This is usually hidden by the children and has to be redeemed by the celebrant with a gift.

Bar Mitzwah: The coming of age of a Jewish boy at the age of 13, when he reads a chapter of the Torah during the Sabbath service. From then on, he is expected to observe all Jewish religious duties. Bar means son, mitzwah is duty.

Bath Mitzwah: Jewish girls did not have such an initiation, but insisted in modern time, to have a similar ceremony, called Bath Mitzwah (bath means daughter).

Chaluzim: Pioneers, early Jewish settles of Palestine.

Horrah: A Jewish folk dance.

Kashruth: The observance of Jewish dietary laws.

Keren Kajemeth, Keren Hayessod: Jewish National Funds for Israel.

Matzah: The unleavened bread that is eaten during the week of the Passover festival as a reminder of the unleavened bread that the Children of Israel took with them at the time of the exodus from Egypt.

Meshek Hapoaloth: Agricultural school for girls. Meshek means farm. Poel is a worker; Poaloth are female workers.

Shavuoth: The Jewish feast of Pentecost, remembering the giving of the ten commandents to Moses, and the harvest of the first fruits.

Simchath Torah: The joy of the Torah, the feast on the eighth day of Succoth, when the last chapter of the Torah is read followed by the first chapter of the new cycle.

Succoth: The feast of thanksgiving of the harvest. During the week of this holiday, observant Jews live in flimsy huts with roofs made out of branches as a reminder of the huts in which the Children of Israel were living during their wanderings in the desert after the exodus from Egypt.

Verein fuer den Klassischen Chorgesang: A choir who performed at concerts of classical music. The members paid a membership fee. Only soloists got paid.

Wandervogel: A German youth organization that hiked throughout Germany, was deeply patriotic, and shunned alcohol, smoking, and ballroom dancing.

Yom Kippur: The Day of Atonement, a day of fasting, the highest Jewish holiday.

Youth Aliyah: Aliyah means ascend and is used for immigration to the Holy Land. Youth aliyah is an organization, founded by Henrietta Szold, to bring Jewish children to schools in Israel to save them from persecution, especially during the Nazi regime in Germany.

ABOUT THE AUTHOR

The first year in Palestine was a heartbreaking disappointment. My body could not take the harsh reality of a life of hard work under primitive living conditions. Besides asthma, I suffered from hepatitis, huge infected boils and dysentery. Just as I began to feel better, I fell from a horse and hurt my lower back. Finally, my doctor, and my companions, advised me to move to Jerusalem, which had a better climate. In Jerusalem, I made a meager living as maid, cook, and nanny. I felt that I was a failure and regretted that I could not live up to my ideals.

But during that year of 1935, I also met Jacob Orfali, a great Armenian young man, now gray, but still young, with whom I have shared my life since then.

It was a difficult decision to marry a non-Jew, but my family supported me, and accepted him as an esteemed member of the family. My three brothers, my parents and Aunt Hede were able to escape from Germany to Jerusalem.

During the Israeli War of Independence, Jacob took me and our three children to his Aunt Justine, a nun in a convent in Bethlehem. After the armistice, Bethlehem became a part of Jordan. So we lived for three years in Arab territory. Jacob lost his job as an auditor for the Sacony Vacuum Oil Company and worked as a teacher of business education and modern languages at Brothers College in Jerusalem until his old firm called him for work in Damascus. From there, he moved to Beirut to work for the United Nations, where we could join him. By now our family was complete with four children, George, Gabrielle, Joseph Sebastian, and John.

Jacob saw trouble brewing in Lebanon and decided to move to the first country that would accept us as immigrants. That country was Brazil.

We stayed in Sao Paulo for 5 years. Jacob had good jobs but the opportunities for the education of our four children were quite insufficient. Jacob wanted to go to the United States, but I did not want to leave my Brazilian friends. I had finally felt at home in Brazil after a difficult period of adjustment.

Nevertheless, we left Brazil in March, 1957 to join Jacob's aunt in Chicago, who had sponsored us.

We lived through good and bad times, gave a good education to our children, who are all happy and successful. Gabrielle, now Mrs. Frank Scaccia, a hospital administrator, gave us two wonderful grandchildren. George and John are systems analysts and Sebastian is a publisher.

I finally continued my education and became a social studies teacher in elementary school, then a teacher of German and French in high school. I enjoyed studying so much that I continued to get a masters degree in guidance and counseling after I had earned my bachelor's degree.

After my retirement, I wrote a book, "Second Goal", a crime story, set in Brazil, using our own experiences in a lower-middle class suburb in Sao Paulo. It was published in 1976 by And/Or Press, Berkeley.

When Jacob retired, we moved to Napa, California, where we currently reside.

———————●———————